So You Want to be a Missionary, Too?

• • • • •

Behind the Missionary Smile

• • • •

By Don Mingo

Copyright © Donald James Mingo 2024
ISBN: 979-8-9874764-1-3
Published in September 2024
Mingo Coaching Group LLC
Grandbury, Texas USA
donmingobooks@gmail.com
Proofreading by: Kathy Mingo
Cover Design by Daniel Mingo

While each account in this book is true, some names and identifying details have been changed to protect the privacy of individuals.

Table of Contents

Dedication

This latest work is written by a missionary, to missionaries, about missionary stuff. You're an elite group of people. After Jesus, our Great Champion and Perfecter of Faith, you are the unrecognized heroes of the Church.

You're a significant extension of a local church's fulfillment of the Great Commission, which is to *make disciples of all nations;* the completion of the Acts 1:8 model, *and to the ends of the earth.*

Missionaries, no one knows or understands the Gospel trenches like you. Your pain is often profound, and the scars you carry testify to your faithfulness.

May you feel appreciated and loved in the following pages.

What's in a Smile, Anyways?

A smile is a most intriguing, mysterious messenger of so many emotions and intentions. It shares the most enjoyable pleasantries with another or dashes and rips away a person's feelings of belonging.

Smiles erupt in expressions of happiness, surprise, or enchantment. With a simple smile, reassurance gently nudges you forward or says, "Why bother? I don't have a chance."

A smile can offer suggestive interconnecting embraces, bringing a person into another's emotional circle.

Or... it becomes a conduit for messaging disappointment or regret.

Hopelessness exudes from the muscles of the face, declaring, "I'm finished. I've lost. There's nowhere to go from here."

Smiles can provide excellent camouflage, too. Hiding in the privacy of emotions, a smile puts people off the scent of emotional distress, distancing, and injury.

Acting as a spy, a smile garners someone's trust, only to discover later it was a ruse, a betrayal.

Deceiving smiles—a weapon of choice—can lead to emotional desolation, as it robs someone of their wealth, trust, or happiness.

A smile can embrace you in friendship or stick a knife in the back.

A smile:

Makes people laugh.

Makes em scared, too.

Communicates politeness.

Condescension.

Frustration.

And... smiles often contain subtitles, too.

We're not very good at parsing a smile from its captions—what is really going on behind the smile.

Ever misread a smile?

So many variables.

There's that phony smile—until, perhaps, you discover behind that strange fake constriction of the face is a person with Multiple Sclerosis whose brain no longer communicates with the nerves of the face, making a 'normal' smile impossible.

Whatever a normal smile is, anyway.

A smiley face icon in a text message says...

Smiles communicate love, compassion, enjoyment, surprise, or intrigue.

One of the most enjoyable smiles as an observer of people is the expression on a parent's face when a child laughs.

But really, what exactly is in a smile, particularly the missionary smile?

Missionaries, we've become quite proficient smilers. We hide many hurts, struggles, and desolating disappointments behind them. Don't we?

Physically, a smile is nothing more than a facial expression formed primarily by flexing the muscles at the sides of the mouth.[1]

It's said that there are nineteen different smiles, but only six show happiness.[2]

Hum, only six.

Wonder what the other thirteen smiles are for?

Some smiles produce endorphins, which help to block pain.

They can also aid in feeling pleasure.

A smile sends signals stimulating the brain's reward system, too.[3]

The muscle movement in a smile stimulates the Amygdala, which releases neurotransmitters to help you adopt an emotionally cheerful disposition.[4]

Duchenne De Boulogne, a 19th-century pioneer in neurology and medical photography, is famous for his discovery of the genuine, often involuntary smile of happiness, which perhaps displays the sincere authenticity of a smile.[5]

Psychologists refer to this smile as the Duchenne smile, involving higher cheek raising.[6] They continue to study it some two hundred years later.[7]

Then, to me, there are smiles of the inner soul—that mysterious quality still lacking complete comprehension of what's happening inside the real person—the real me the actual you.

Herman Melville, the author of *Moby Dick,* wrote, "A smile is the chosen vehicle of all ambiguities."[8]

Shakespeare penned in his poem, *Venus and Adonis*, "A smile cures the wounding of a frown."

Often attributed to Mark Twain, it was American writer Christian Nestell Bovee who wrote, "Kindness, a language which the dumb can speak, and the deaf can understand." [9,10,11]

In the Book of Psalms, the Sons of Korah sang, "Truth springs up from the earth, and righteousness smiles down from heaven,".[12]

But now, here, it's the missionary smile that intrigues me. It's a quality I've deliberately observed for many years. What makes it unique, at least to me, is the adventurous, exploratory nature behind it: the missionary life. There is nothing like it.

To willingly leave family and home, begging for the money to do so, hauling your spouse and three little children to a place you barely understand, learn a language that seems impossible, endure sicknesses you've never seen before, overlook slurs, never able to be a full-part of any circle of friends, and yet, to experience the marvelous encounters that no one 'back home' can comprehend or cares to hear about. That's the missionary life.

There's the adventure.

Helping someone who otherwise would not receive it.

To sing in another language, Zulu in my case.

Acquiring a worldview that few will ever grasp.

Through language acquisition, cognitive abilities develop beyond those of monolinguals.

To sing in another language.

To think in three languages, it's quite a thing.

The exquisite tastes of other cultural foods.

Those mountains.

The seas.

A herd of elephants passing by as you sip coffee on the porch of a coffee shop in Kolhapur, India.

Deep sea fishing in the Indian Ocean.

Enjoying a scone and cup of tea, viewing the Swiss Alps from a balcony.

Traveling over the Andes Mountains.

Sharing Matte Tea with an acquaintance in Paraguay.

Standing on a flat-roof balcony in India observing the goings-on of people below.

Viewing the Illuminated Manuscripts in the British Museum

Seeing a mummy up close.

Those Assyrian tablets; I could've spent a month there.

Drinking coffee from the top of the Eiffel Tower.

Have I ever told you I like coffee?

Standing at Cape Point, Africa witnessing the clear distinction of the green warmer waters of the Indian Ocean meeting the blue colder waters of the Atlantic.

Oh, and the penguins, too.

Enjoying our twentieth wedding anniversary sitting on a bench observing Victoria Falls in Zimbabwe, Africa.

A huge boomslang snake fell from a tree above us and landed twenty feet away.

Won't forget that anniversary, especially after a security guard ran up and blew it to pieces with a shotgun not fifty feet from us.

Our 20th anniversary went off with a bang.

Seeing the Colosseum in Rome.

Eating food at a Thai street cafe in Bangkok.

Seeing the Laughing Buddha.

Observing Hindus at the Festival of Ganesh Chaturthi in India.

Flying over the mountains of South Africa and Lesotho.

Leading exchange students on ten-day hikes through the mountains.

Scuba diving in Sodwana Bay in the Indian Ocean.

Then, there are the friendships. Those many friendships missionary service affords.

For me, walking into a completely different culture of people, finding acceptance and belonging simply because we share an affinity: Jesus Christ.

The best? Seeing someone bury their faith in Jesus Christ who responded to our ministry and message.

The missionary life. There is none like it. So, too, the missionary smile.

Whatever a missionary smile is, like an archaeologist, I've tried to unearth it because so many secrets lie behind it.

Behind those smiles we generate is where the actual battle takes place. Conflicts that few see or understand. Struggles we choose to conceal from others and often ourselves. Concealed from others, we hide an inner person that few missionaries ever share.

Our missionary smiles protect us. Betray us, too, when holding indefensible positions behind walls of self-deception that say, "All is well," when it's not.

The SS Missionary Calling is seaworthy, and once resupplied, you're ready to set sail. However, an unrealized fact is that sometimes fissures in the soul's hull allow leaking, bringing doubt, discouragement, and disqualification to flood our lower decks of spiritual vitality and life.

Then, in the open waters of ministry, in the seas of spiritual warfare, hearts and intents flounder as cracks hidden behind many a missionary's smile open, incapacitating us as our compromised keel shows gaping fissures of emotions.

What lies behind our smiles? It's here we win or lose.

Those Missionary Smiles

A MESSAGE AWAITED ME IN my inbox that morning. A single female missionary talked with us many times as we bumped into each other on the missionary trail.

As she shared her missionary journey, we'd become friends with Olivia—not her real name.

Over the course of fifteen years, Olivia changed fields of service several times. The challenges she faced as a single female missionary seemed overwhelming. We corresponded often.

Then, I read an email one morning. The title read, ***"Behind the Missionary Smile."***

In a quick note, she suggested, "You know, Don, write a book called *Behind the Missionary Smile."*

She continued, "When missionaries stand before potential supporters, report to current financial contributors, or give reports to mission agencies, family, and friends, they often do so behind a smile that says, 'Everything is wonderful. I'm at the top of my game, and the ministry is going great! All is okay. I'm okay. My ministry is worth your support.'"

Yeah, right.

"Most of the time, I'm not doing so well behind that smile of mine. There is loneliness, heartbreak, betrayal, and other stuff going on that I never mention... that we can't mention. Stuff we cover with a smile because it's just too shameful, embarrassing, or painful to divulge. And I can't remember the last time I wasn't sick."

She finished, "Besides, who really cares anyway? Right?"

My mind started churning. How many missionaries live and serve in self-imposed isolation, hiding their hurts and perceived shortcomings behind skillfully acquired smiles from years of practice and training.

Always put your best foot forward. Remember, convince everyone that what you're doing is worth their financial contributions to your ministry.

Those Smiles in Europe

In that same month, 500 miles away, we sat before a couple giving a report of their European ministry to an American church. Hardly an empty chair existed as a large group attended the evening service.

Living and serving there for almost twenty years, they glowed, sharing all 'the great things God is doing in our ministry.'

They impressed me in so many ways.

Afterward, Kathy and I joined the Missionary Fellowship. Here, members could get to know 'their missionaries' better. An hour later, after many left, it was our turn.

I was so looking forward to a mutually enriching conversation, and offered, "That was quite a report you gave tonight. Wow, amazing ministry you've got there."

Can you believe the exact next comment that followed?

She began, "Well, yes, it was our furlough report. But behind our smiles is another world we never share. It's another story altogether."

Tears filled this woman's eyes as she spoke. Then she immediately dropped her head with closed eyes.

That comment, *'Behind the smile,'* made in the same month by two missionaries from two separate mission agencies serving in entirely different cultures, hung unto me.

Ten minutes into the conversation, after learning Kathy and I were in missionary care, the wife expressed more pain and discontent. She continued, "When they recruited us as missionaries, they presented only the best parts of missionary life. Those who accompanied us pushed many idealistic expectations of what a 'good missionary couple like us could accomplish on this field.'"

We were just kids. What did we know? Hadn't been married more than a year yet.

You know what?

Most of what they told us was an outright lie or ignorant misinformation, blah, blah, blah, blah...

No one discussed how difficult and depressing it would be to live and raise a family in Europe as a missionary.

And... the struggles to raise financial support, then keeping that support any time a church at some whim considered dropping us. It never ends.

A bunch of tourists from our church talked us into going. They were really only interested in gaining one more trophy for their missionary showcase. Look at all the missionaries we support!

And our mission agency is just after the money. You know, they now take 15% of our support every month to pay their staff, and they live considerably better than we do.

We raise the money; they take the money. That's what it all seems to come down to.

She looked away, 'Missionary life is lonelier than anyone ever told me.'

Whew… Before us sat 'successful' missionaries caught in a perfect storm of emotional drift, battered and blown about by unexpected and unprepared for winds of missionary life.

Laden down by perceptions of betrayal and unable to find their true North, they despaired. Behind their smiles, turbulent waves of despondency lay—waves that few knew existed.

Those conversations hang on me. It comes to mind often, more so when writing these pages.

We know these feelings.

Behind our smiles exist hurts, doubts, and uncertainties.

How do we deal with it?

How do you deal with it?

What's behind a smile, anyway?

13

14

The Lost Tribe of Missionary Smiles

Inactive, retired, or retreating Sent Ones often scatter our Church's landscapes far out of view. Some serving in isolation away from a team of encouragers gave up, retreating far behind the front lines unnoticed, uncared for, and unengaged.

Others suffering from chronic illnesses, radioing back home, "All is well," disappeared into the horizons of missionary life.

Some hide out. They're still 'missionaries,' but they rarely do missionary work. Vacillating in empty idleness, they live on the field while accepting sacrificial donations from their supporters.

Then, there's the missionary couple that's in trouble. Seen this situation too many times. A sudden resignation only to learn that a long-hidden trail of infidelity ended a marriage.

Or another missionary kid who, upon leaving home, crashes and burns, unable to adjust to their parent's country of birth.

And those after returning 'home,' found it impossible to adjust to their passport countries they once belonged to, now seeming more foreign than the field they served in.

Returning with throbbing experiences of pain, they became part of the once-upon-a-time tribe of missionaries, mass casualties of the Church.

Forgotten heroes, much like those in the military who served on the front lines of battle. However, once they leave the field, most missionaries don't get follow-up care, combat pay, pensions, medical insurance, or mental health care.

Sent Ones, 'giving their all,' quickly fade from overfilled church schedules, overlooked by the busy lives that once supported them. Perhaps unaware because their smiles communicated, "All is well," as their lives sank into an abyss of defeat, finding themselves in the backwaters of aloneness.

Active missionaries struggling to navigate the windy depths of missionary service, life, and reentry.

We rarely discuss such crossings or put them in our updates to supporters.

Do we?

Missionaries?

Huh?

But they're there, and we know they're there because we are there. We just can't or refuse to recognize them. Perhaps our biggest challenge is what's behind all those smiles.

What All These Smiles Have in Common

All these missionaries bear a commonality. In their ministries, fundraising, report giving, and work, they stood behind smiles, relaying a message,

ALL IS WELL...

I know this from observation, countless sessions with missionaries, and...well...from myself, too. Sometimes, even now, I find myself there again. Hiding behind a smoke screen smile of:

- No one's going to know how much pain I'm in today.

- How infuriated I am with the neighbor's continual pounding music penetrating my house at all hours of the night.

- Anger after another person tells me that my Muscular Dystrophy could be cured if I took these vitamins, tried a bottle of blue-green algae, Shaklee, Herbalife, Essential Oils, and...well, I'm crabby now.

Hey! But still smiling!

Now, this book is not an expose of the casualties of missionary service, although perhaps one should be written someday.

Or about the weakness of church and missions agencies that superbly recruit missionaries, 'train them,' sends them out to share the Good News of Jesus Christ, but…as they fade into the horizons of their new ventures, drift from memory and care.

Fortunately, several agencies, such as my own, have started constructing missionary retirement villages for faithful workers reaching their golden years. This added to an ever increasing missionary care program to help our missionaries.

For this I am truly thankful.

Yet, many head to the Gospel trenches unprepared, without spiritual and physical medics, armed with their smiles, but with almost zero understanding of what awaits them.

These are the casualties of Gospel warfare—sharing Jesus, the Way, the Truth, and the Life.

We can talk with other missionaries about our experiences because they bear the same scars. Missionaries are our people. They understand. They get it.

But talking with civilians or someone who's not seen more than a mission trip or two brings about a different, more neutral conversation because, frankly, missionary tourists don't know what we're talking about or what they're talking about most of the time when it comes to missionary life.

To them, we often leave the impression that we're bragging—or worse, lying—when just sharing a memory.[14] This is because only a missionary's people can fathom missionary life. We are part of the missionary tribe.

Hopefully

This book is for you. For the few who will ever read it—I'm not a well-recognized writer, plus I write to a very narrow niche—I pray that the following pages will encourage and help you deal with the realities of missionary life, your life.

As we embark upon each chapter of our missionary journey, may we see Christ amid stormy headwinds. This voyage is often tumultuous, but as a fellow sailor who've navigated these waters, remember that our Captain, the Way, the Truth, and the Life, provides a beacon of hope leading us to our Anchor of Rest.

What's behind those smiles?

Lingering
Loneliness

I pray that no missionary will ever be as lonely as I have been.[15]

—Lottie Moon
Missionary to China 1893-1912

THE DIRECTOR OF A LARGE mission agency recently shared, "Our missionary women cite loneliness as their number one problem."

I thought, "Yes, that's problematic. Loneliness plagues many missionaries and debilitates them when left unchecked."

Yesterday, I read on my Facebook page a post by a thirty-year missionary veteran titled "Sometimes it's lonely…" This, from a man in his late fifties.

Loneliness is part of the human experience in which few are exempt.

Missionary loneliness—well… that's another thing altogether. The lifestyle, calling, and demands can swell into an overwhelming sense of aloneness because we are never completely with 'our own kind.'

Are we?

How do we deal with our loneliness? Is there a way to ease the abandonment of aloneness when our needs for social interaction go unmet?

Loneliness, Not Just a Missionary Problem

According to many mental health professionals, loneliness is a problem worldwide.

Dr. Vivek Murthy, the U.S. Surgeon General, is outspoken about loneliness's mental and physical health effects. In 2023, he issued an advisory on the healing effects of social connection and community.[16]

> The harmful consequences of a society that lacks social connection can be felt in our schools, workplaces, and civic organizations, where performance, productivity, and engagement are diminished," the advisory reads.[17]

In our social media connective societies, loneliness appears greater than ever.

Robin Price entered missionary service in Ukraine in 2014. She shared her battle with loneliness.

> I allowed the loneliness to turn my gaze inward and focus on what I DON'T have. I allowed it to feed my desire for comfort and even for a spouse, for a mere man rather than for God Himself. And I floundered for a while, my joy dwindling away. Where was the goodness of God—that rich provision that I had experienced throughout my journey to get here? And I began to turn to temporary "fixes" (e.g., movies, food).[18]

Loneliness often comes as a soft whisper in the night. In a crowd of people murmuring, "Hey, you're all alone here. No one wants to connect with you, really. Oh, they'll be kind, but there's a line of friendship you'll not be able to cross. After all, you're a missionary."

During our second furlough, a leader in the church we called 'Home Church' said, "I'm not getting close to you and Kathy because, in a year, you'll be back in South Africa. I don't have time for that."

It stings to this day.
Deceiving thoughts.
They don't care.
No one thinks about us.
They just want to use us.
We're just numbers for their missions program.
We'll never have genuine friends.
Better get used to it.
You're by yourself, with yourself, and on your own.
Buck up.
But radiate that smile up if you want those funds to continue.

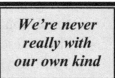

We're never really with our own kind

The Alone Whisperer

Aloneness whispers into the soul's ear unhealthy utterances. As an unwelcomed guest in the missionary wilderness, loneliness softly plants seeds of:

- Your faith is weak.
- You're unworthy.
- You're alone.
- You'll always be alone.
- Nobody cares about your pain.
- You're not one of them.
- No one thinks about you.
- Zero people understand and, once more, don't care.
- You'll always ache like this.
- You will always feel this way.[19]
- Go ahead, lose yourself in the internet world of…

- Those images will cover your pain.
- You'll forget about your loneliness when with your internet 'friends.'
- Go ahead and double up on your meds. That recommended dosage is only a suggestion.
- Numb yourself.
- Find an escape.
- You'll always be single.
- Take that drink. It's not like anyone's here to see you do it.
- Swallow that pill.
- Spend most of your time doing anything other than what you tell your supporters you do.
- Do you really think you'll make a friend here?
- Only closed doors await you back home.
- Hang a big 'closed' sign over your feelings.
- They've forgotten about you.
- No place will ever feel like home again.
- You're destitute of any meaningful roots.
- You're unneeded, unwanted, and undesirable.
- Introduce yourself to Emptiness; here's your companion.
- No one wants you in the group.
- Go ahead, hurt yourself. It's ok because that pain covers up your greatest pain: loneliness.
- So, cut yourself.
- Throw yourself into that wall.
- Hit yourself again, it's ok. It numbs you to your real pain.
- Have that panic attack; everything is beyond your control.
- Besides, you're a lousy friend-maker, anyway. Always have been.
- You've got so little to offer.
- People don't like you because…
- You can't blend in anyhow.
- Welcome to rejection. I'm your new home.
- Be angry with God. This is how he pays you back for serving.

- This is the missionary life. Get used to it.
- I'll never be far away—Loneliness.
- Just fake being ok, otherwise…
- *Ah, Look at All the Lonely People.*
- Alone now.
- Alone tomorrow.
- Always alone.
- *Home Alone* without the happy ending.
- So, give it up.
- "Hello darkness, my old friend…"[20]

But remember to smile when back home in front of all those supporters. A smile brings the ka-ching! Besides, no one likes a whiner.

Does any of this resonate with you? Look, we all experience isolation in our lives, right? That's part of the missionary experience.

But when isolation turns from a sense of aloneness into distressing experiences, bringing intense feelings of emptiness, pain, and emotional heaviness,[21] that's when we're in trouble.

Signs of Unhealthy Aloneness

Here are some considerations. No one condition means you're suffering from the adverse effects of chronic loneliness, but if five or more of these apply, well then… please take note.

- You constantly feel tired.
- You're consumed with buying and selling.
- Acquire more stuff, and then get rid of it.
- Spend much of your time binge-watching TV shows.
- Devoting way…… too much time on social media.
- Overreacting.
- Weight gain.
- You always feel sick.[22]

23

- Cold or flu-like symptoms that linger longer than usual.
- Headaches, body aches, and insomnia or hypersomnia.
- Focusing attention mostly inwardly.
- Fixating on physical symptoms you would have otherwise ignored or brushed off in the past.[23]
- Zero close friends.
- Chronic feelings of isolation when surrounded by others or in large groups.
- Feelings of not being good enough.
- Shallow interactions with others.
- "I'm the least-liked person in the group."
- Avoidance of people.
- You experience exhaustion and burnout when socializing with others.[24]

Dealing With Missionary Loneliness

How do we deal with loneliness? I'd like to tell you, just pray and read the Bible a little more, suck it up, get tough, and deal with it. But you're already doing that. Aren't you?

Perhaps there's more to it than following a chart and checking off boxes of spiritual disciplines to compensate for loneliness.

Or confess that loneliness is a sinful lack of trust in God, weak faith, and a poor spiritual constitution because... spiritual people aren't lonely. Right?

That's not what the Bible indicates. After his Facebook friends visited to 'encourage' him, Job cried out, "...so I am allotted *months of emptiness*, and nights of misery are apportioned to me." Job 7:3 ESV

In his book, *The Anatomy of Loneliness*, Thomas Wolfe writes, "The most tragic, sublime and beautiful expression of loneliness which I have ever read is the Book of Job."[25]

24

Ever been there? Wonder how lonely Joseph became during all those days in prison?

Or Hannah, continually crying out for a son?

Elijah as he ran from Queen Jezebel in his dilapidated condition?

Moses, during his years of exile in the desert?

David, who spent years running from King Saul, hiding in the caves of Israel?

And what about Jesus? Hebrews 4:15

The Bible doesn't condemn loneliness. Instead, it encourages us to look beyond our loneliness and embrace intimacy by grasping onto God's promises—I will never leave you or forsake you. Then, activate God's network of saints.[26]

And let us not neglect our meeting together, as some people do, but encourage one another, especially now that the day of his return is drawing near. Hebrews 10:25

Some practicable suggestions. Take the helpful ones and ignore those that don't apply. If you disagree with a point or two, no problem; ignore them. Okay?

When I go out to eat, I usually bypass anything with red meat on the menu. Beef is not nice to me. However, I don't throw the entire menu away; instead, I choose what agrees with my weak constitution.

So, let's look at the menu here.

Admit you're lonely. I don't believe loneliness is a sin. There's no shame in being lonely. Many missionaries think so. Like, if I admit I'm lonely… Well, okay, what, then?

Our reactions to loneliness may lead us to sin, but loneliness itself is a common human emotion.

You're normal.

How about that?

You're not The Supermissionary able to abstain from human emotions.

I don't think loneliness is a sign of some deficiency in character and soul, either.

The question becomes, "How do we deal with our loneliness?

Missionaries, we chronically ignore major issues to the detriments of ourselves.

Don't we?

Well, we're on a God mission, right?

"I don't have time to be lonely."

Yeah, until loneliness bites you in your emotional sitzfleisch as you crawl up a tree of self-denial, hoping you can outwait the Lions of aloneness waiting below.

Then what?

You're stuck in a delusional state, gushing loneliness.

After our first term in South Africa, returning to the States, the last thing I'd acknowledge was my deep, impoverished loneliness. That's not a mark of a spiritual person, right?

Especially a missionary!

And who wants to listen to a missionary drone on about their loneliness? Doesn't build much confidence in prospective supporters either.

Now, our supporters and the churches we share our ministry with treat us with substantial kindness and respect. We're gifted and surrounded by good people.

But occasionally, I'll get a, "Hey, don't complain about loneliness. You chose to be a missionary."

PUNK.

Several months into our first furlough, an acquaintance asked me over a cup of coffee about my life and work in South Africa. Did I ever tell you about how much I love coffee?

Anyway, I replied, "It's a love-hate relationship."

With raised eyebrows, he replied, "What do you mean?"

Deflecting his question, I retorted, "Ah, nothing."

Quite an untruth.

Sometimes, I'm the biggest liar to myself.

So, I limped through fifteen months of grueling reporting and fundraising, returning to the field more alone and emptier than ever.

One thing I didn't do was acknowledge to myself that I needed friendship. My loneliness overlooked the excellent friends we'd gained in Ladysmith, South Africa.

You're not the only one. Almost every missionary I've met who spent considerable time in another culture experiences downhearted lonesomeness.

Knowing that most, if not all, missionaries experience this emotion may console you when staring your loneliness in the eye.

Recently, a single missionary woman serving with medical missions in the Amazon told Kathy, "Loneliness is something I'm finding most missionaries experience. It comes with the territory. I'm trying to learn how to accept and live with it."

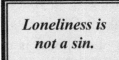

Loneliness is not a sin.

Those are pretty good words there.

Share your loneliness with others who are on a similar journey. The Bible talks a lot about confession. Here, not in the sense of some inward personal sin resulting in exile to the Island of Loneliness.

No, more like Paul suggested to the Galatians, "Share each other's burdens, and in this way obey the law of Christ." Galatians 6:2

And what is the law of Christ? It's the Shema Jesus spoke of when asked, what is the greatest commandment?" Mark 12:30-31

And you must love the Lord your God with all your heart, all your soul, all your mind, and all your strength.' The second is equally important: 'Love your neighbor as yourself.'[Love those around you as you do yourself.

My friend, how can others help you unless you recruit support for the battlefields of lonesomeness?

Talk with other missionaries about your loneliness. Missionaries understand missionary life. Find out how they deal with it.

A burden shared is often a burden carried.

Condition yourself to carry the cross of loneliness. The nature of missionary life incurs aloneness. It comes with the territory.

As we leave family and friends behind for extended periods, the inevitable human cost is isolation. Isolation brings a sense of loneliness. The two are close companions, often traveling together in packs.

Jesus reminds us, "If any of you wants to be my follower, you must give up your own way, take up your cross daily, and follow me." Luke 9:23b

Loneliness is one of those crosses we need to develop a conditioned willingness to carry.

Prepare for it. One huge issue with missionaries' inability to deal with loneliness is that we're not encouraged enough to count the cost of missionary service in terms of loneliness before entering service.

Jesus talked about this.

But don't begin until you count the cost. For who would begin construction of a building without first calculating the cost to see if there is enough money to finish it?

28

Otherwise, you might complete only the foundation before running out of money, and then everyone would laugh at you.

They would say, 'There's the person who started that building and couldn't afford to finish it!'

Luke 14:28-30

Missionary life is often an embattled life. We serve in the trenches of gospel conflict. Loneliness becomes an effective weapon of our enemy, who uses it skillfully to derail us.

Developing your emotional, mental, and spiritual defenses to meet aloneness is a must.

Jesus ended the discussion by saying, *"So you cannot become my disciple without giving up everything you own."* Luke 14:33

Maybe being a missionary disciple of Christ means giving up some connectedness with people in favor of a closer embrace with the Savior. Accept that badge and wear it with honor.

When besieged by loneliness, do something. Because of my Muscular Dystrophy, activities are severely limited. No more kayaking, boating, hunting, fishing, swimming…and you get the picture.

But Don, when loneliness weighs on you, don't just sit there and do nothing! Don't sit and watch TV all day long. DO SOMETHING!

That's one of several reasons I write and self-publish so many books. It helps keep loneliness outside the windows of my heart. Occasionally, I glance out to say, "Loneliness, you're not going to get the best of me. Not today!"

I love to play the guitar and am good at it. When I play my guitars, loneliness crawls away and hides.

But to keep playing with my declining motor skills requires adjustments.

Yesterday, I traded an old guitar and several hundred dollars for a Les Paul-style LTD Deluxe electric guitar. Its long neck and rounded fretboard make chording easier for me. Playing distracts me from loneliness.

Ask yourself, "What's causing me so much loneliness? My loneliness springs from my need for...? How am I going to deal with it?"

Transform loneliness into solitude. Aloneness can become a positive experience.

Solitude presents opportunities to get to know yourself and reflect. It gives time to relax, rest, and contemplate.

To appreciate one's surroundings and focus upon more immediate matters at hand.

Or, as in my case, those many early mornings spent on a high hill behind my house in Ladysmith, South Africa.

Many mornings, empty lots lay below me in the dense fog. Those lots became a vision. Our next ministry project was born. The seeds and inspiration for a $1.6 million new children's care center began on that hill in solitude during the lonely dark morning hours.

Apart from the aloneness that drove me up that hill those mornings, our most crucial ministry project wouldn't have seen the light of day.

Look for serenity in your lonesomeness. Transform loneliness into quietude. Let stillness becomes a virtue of significant gain.

Embrace it and learn to live with it. In this way, we gain the peaceful art of contentment. Finding contentment in loneliness is a virtue of The Cross.

No one experienced more loneliness than Jesus in his last physical days on earth. Abandoned in the Garden by his friends, mocked by the crowd, forsaken by The Father while hanging on that Cross, and cursedly denied by Peter, I'm pretty sure that Jesus understands loneliness.

Loneliness will not go unrewarded. Grab unto this truth. Here's my Facebook message of encouragement to missionaries this past Thanksgiving.

Missionary challenges during the Thanksgiving season, such as being away from family, can be among the loneliest times of the year. May you be blessed as you willingly carry this cross. And know this: 'Great is your reward in heaven.'

 How do you handle your loneliness? Three weeks before my youngest brother Bob died, he called me. We both suffer from the same disease, although his became active almost the minute he was born. Mine didn't start showing signs until my late fifties.

The genetic disorder takes years to inflict maximum damage. I'm beginning to feel and see its effects.

Bob said to me, "I'm worried about you. You're not handling this very well, are you? It's like you're pulling into yourself and shutting the door on everything and everyone else. Brother, you can't tackle this by yourself because alone will leave you alone."

I responded, "Yeah, no worries. I'm ok."

Bob interjected, "Don, stop trying to fake it. This is me. Remember? I know what's going on in your emotions. I know that because you're a missionary and leader, you've got to put on a strong face. Sell yourself to supporters, right?"

He continued, "Listen, there's only one way you'll be able to enjoy life and get through this as the disease eats away at you. And it's going to eat you alive."

Then, I'll never forget his last words to me.

Openings for appreciation surround you. Every morning, when you get up, take a second and look around. What's in front of you that causes appreciation?

After a brief discussion, Bob concluded, "You can hide behind a smile, refusing to let anyone into your world of pain and loss, living in secret misery. Or get on board the Boat of Appreciation; it's a choice. Take it from me; I know there's enough pain with this disease without adding more to yourself."

As he struggled to breathe, "There's more to appreciate than depreciate, even as this enemy pounds us every day. Find gratitude and focus on it every moment of every day. You can live a meaningful life in contentment, even in all the pain and weakness coming your way. But you'll never make it by yourself. You'll only be agonizingly lonely."

"Search for it, brother, get hold of it."

A few days later, Bob inherited a body that will never fail him again as Jesus ushered him into eternal life.

> *Developing your emotional, mental, and spiritual defenses to meet loneliness is a must.*

Appreciation is a loneliness-killer. Nothing calms the deep, dark, icy waters of loneliness more than gratitude.

Like a gold miner, look deep behind your smile. Dig out appreciation's nuggets of gold. Then, when loneliness creeps out of your Mordor,[27] let Isildur[28] depower the beast, slaying it in its tracks.

Loneliness submits to gratitude, removing itself from the power seat of your emotions.

Moving Forward: Don't beat yourself up. We all experience the lonesomeness of loneliness. Have you ever considered that perhaps your loneliness is an intimate mark of identification with our Savior?

> He was *despised* and *rejected—*
>   a man of *sorrows*, acquainted with *deepest grief.*
> We turned our backs on him and looked the other way.
>   He was despised, and we did not care.
>
> Isaiah 53:3

Remember

Jesus experienced loneliness, too. You're never alone, ever. Look around. The friends God brings your way may surprise you if you can just see them.

Remember, you've got to be a friend to gain a friend. And…our creator promises to never leave us. We are never ever alone.

Ever.

No matter how alone we feel.

Turn to me and be gracious to me,
for <u>I</u> <u>am</u> <u>lonely</u> and afflicted.

Psalm 25:16 NIV

Erratic
Expectations

IN MY LAST BOOK FOR MISSIONARIES, I spent considerable time on the often emotional career-ending experience of dealing with unmet expectations.

Missionary expectations can appear as inconsistent, unpredictable wishes of desire or demand. As an advocate for missionaries, my primary concern is for you. When a missionary comes off the field prematurely because something or someone didn't meet anticipations of what missionary life should look like, a struggle with that decision exists long after leaving missionary work.

> **Expectation is the graveyard of many Missionary callings.**

Sometimes, missionaries self-deceive, convincing themselves of a story with impossible odds that forced them off the field. Trying to ease their conscience, they live in the backwaters of their own untruths. "This didn't work out, that didn't work out, and it wasn't like we expected."

Hey, the good news...God's grace is overwhelmingly more than enough to give you worth in reassessing your expectations. 'Missionary' does not define you; Jesus does.

Over my 30-plus years of missionary service, I've heard at least a dozen times from pastors and their wives, who used to be missionaries, share self-delusional stories about why they left the field.

Voices processed through my head, "Who are you trying to convince here?"

Unmet expectations are the graveyard of many missionary call-ings. Hear it all the time.

"I came off the field because it wasn't at all like I thought it would be."

My usual response is, "What did you think missionary life would be like?"

The answer often goes something like, "I don't know, just not like that."

 What's behind an expectation, anyway? Isn't it birthed from a desire for something or someone to act in a man-ner that pleases and accommodates you? And what hap-pens when that accommodation fails to appear?

An expectation: a firm belief that future events and results will conform to inward thoughts of, *"This is the way it should be, it must be, to be the way I want it to be, or…else."*

Right?

How else would there be such high defections from missionary ranks otherwise? A missionary's reason,

"I left the field because…it wasn't…"

Expectation springs from deep within our emotions. Once breached, misperceptions leak in, compromising expectation's bulk-heads and sinking a missionary's calling and career. This can nega-tively affect missionaries for the rest of their lives. I've seen this more times than I can count.

And where do those expectations come from? Don't they form from our thoughts and experiences within our own cultural back-yards?

This is how it must be! How it better be; or else.

36

In operating through an ethnocentric viewpoint, we see things in our ethos, churches, training, and understanding of what missions should look like.

Right?

No?

Sure, we do.

We arrive on the field expecting missionary relations to favor us.

Housing will occur to our satisfaction.

Within a year, we'll master the country's language, speaking with complete fluency.

The children will quickly adjust.

Then, the people of that country will, no, must line up to follow our vision for the work WE'RE going to build.

Like pawns on the chessboards, we move them about to make ministry work.

Whose ministry?

Right?

No?

Let's consider this.

To what extent do most missionaries spend significant time with a country's people before embarking on missionary service there?

Could it be that the blueprints for missionary work are often crafted with a narrow focus, based on missionary specificity, before stepping foot in the field? Our own cultural norms become the yard-stick against which we measure the 'nationals.'

So then, don't expectations become driving forces to bend people and situations to our will? You know, the way these people must think and act to make a ministry successful?

An old pastor once told me **three things about expectations**. I've never forgotten them. He said, "I know what you're expecing in ministry, but…"

1. With the number of people on this planet, no matter how big or how many people sit under your ministry, mathematically, the percentage of your people compared to the world's population is zero. So, **don't become proud**.

2. Sometimes, that's the best people can do. So **don't expect more** than people can give.

3. No matter what you say or do to persuade people, **people will always do what they want to do**, regardless.

Expectations sink many missionaries when people don't conform to their moorings of ministry.

And really, what do we control?

Only the Creator possesses absolute power to control.

A failed expectation demands, "This and that should have happened this way or that way." Missionaries then return home unaware that their expectations became idols, something they put before God.

Expectancy Over Expectation

What about, instead of expectation, we develop a wide-ranging attitude of **expectancy**?

Expectation says, "It must be this way."

Expectancy points expectation towards another direction with much more flexibility.

I like this definition: *"**Expectancy** is the feeling or hope that something exciting, interesting, or good is about to happen."*[29]

It's an expectation without the specificity of **'this is how it must be.'**

Expectancy Anticipates...

Meeting people who live and think differently from us.

Trying and tasting new foods. I still miss koeksisters, boerewors, puddings, biltong, Bovril, and other foods I enjoyed during our many years in South Africa.

Anticipation of new experiences you will come across.

Vacations on the Indian Ocean.

Making new friends.

New adventures.

Sharing the loving hope for this world, Jesus

Expectancy places the responsibility upon God's faithfulness to deliver. Expectation pressures you to mold events, places, and people into your image of what things should look like.

Expectancy takes a lot of pressure off the missionary.

How might you temper your expectations toward a more God-centered view of expectancy? Expecting great things from God rather than trying to press surroundings into your desires presents a much healthier option.

It's exciting, too!

Seeing God accomplish things we couldn't network on our best day brings far more enthusiasm and productivity.

Piloting your ministry on expectations drives one into rocks of frustration and disappointment.

Serving with expectancy encourages an enriching attitude that helps cut through life's storms far more efficiently ultimately bringing us into safe harbors of thought and emotions.

Moving Forward: On two columns of paper, computer, or smartphone, mark one column MY EXPECTATION and the other MY EXPECTANCY. Fill both columns. What do you see?

Remember

Expect God to work, but let the Captain guide your dreams, desires, and demands. In this, you'll always weather expectations' gales of disappointments. Expectancy in God to work removes the pressure off you to perform; make something happen.

Expectancy remembers, "He who has begun a good work in you will complete it until the day of Jesus Christ…" Philippians 1:6 NKJV

My soul, wait silently for God alone,
For my expectation *is* from Him.

Psalms 62:5 NKJV

Certain
Uncertainties

They were to present their ministry that Sunday morning and the somewhat expected unexpected happened just twenty minutes from the church.

Little Denny blew his diaper out, and his four-year-old brother, Donnie, sat in his car seat whining, "I don't want to go!"

The middle brother, Dannie, sat between the two in his usually introverted manner, staring at his Radio Shack Race Way handheld game without a peep.

Just minutes before the mayhem broke out in the back seat, missionary Dad and mom got into it. Dad always freaked out a bit when running late, as they were. Mom tolerated a difficult night with a migraine. The two together mixed into an emotional uneasiness.

Here's mom bringing a hazmat team into the back seat to deal with little Denny's fecal eruption, which now covers his hands, car seat, and the window next to him.

Dad is panicking because they're ten minutes behind their required arrival time.

Donnie is still a bit fussy.

Dannie continues sitting between the two, staring at his game.

And mom…she's still battling a painful eruption in her head that three Tylenol barely touched.

Upon entering that small church, the pastor stood waiting for them. With beaming smiles on their faces, they greeted the pastor.

Good morning, pastor! It is such an honor to be with you today. We look forward to sharing our ministry and field with your fine people.

Mom reaffirmed with a forced, believable smile. The pastor stood clueless about the havoc that broke out in the car that morning, before arriving in the church's parking lot.

With that, Dad hastened to set up their missionary display as Mom dragged their three little boys into the bathroom to finish making them presentable.

The family, all smiling—well…a forced smile—but they all got through the service that morning.

After lunch, the pastor announced, "Our church will be taking you on for monthly financial support."

Mom and Dad left the diner smiling, climbing into the car with Denny, who needed another diaper changed. Donnie wound up on sugar, having received too many sweets in Sunday School, and Dannie still not saying much.

With Mom feeling the migraine returning and Dad collapsing into the driver's seat in fatigue, they made their way back to a missionary apartment three hours away.

This was just one Sunday morning account of us, the Mingo family. Whenever I've shared this story with missionaries, as I did this week at Advanced Missionary Training before twenty recruits, heads nod up and down with giggles, affirming a camaraderie of similar experiences.

It's something only missionaries can relate to.

ONE THING SURE ABOUT MISSIONARY life is that it's filled with uncertainties. Over the years, prospective and seasoned missionaries shared their lack of sureness about their many uncertainties. Perhaps you'd like to highlight which uncertainties relate to you:

How sure am I about…?
Am I cut out for missionary life?
What will our/my parents say?
And my friends…?
How do you become a missionary?
What do I need to do?
What about seeking support?
Can I get everything I need to live on the field?
I don't know about the educational requirements…
Will I ever be able to learn the language?
Do I even need to learn the language?
What does my mission agency expect of me?
Who will be on the team I'm assigned to?
What if I don't like the leader of that team?
How can we afford our children's schooling?
What about my aging, frail parents back home?
Our first child going off to university…?
What about visa uncertainties?
Can we get adequate care for our autistic child?
What's the new government's attitude towards missionaries?
How do we deal with the unrest in the country?
The rising crime levels?
The collapse of the government?
Where do you go to get utilities turned on?
How do I post letters and packages where there are no post offices?

Will I ever bond with this new culture?
Is my missionary calling genuine?
Am I going to have to beg for money…
What am I going to do about my depression?
Jesus, is this worth it?
Covid Pandemic Crisis.
Will we ever get this going?
Are we making any difference?
Is Christ really calling me to become a missionary?
What if I get sick…who will…how will I…?
Will we ever be able to return to the field?
And my fears?
What about this mess?
The war…?
Who am I, and what am I doing here?
Can I put up with the new pastor of my sending church?
My loneliness…
The uncertainties of returning home for a leave.
How can I overcome this sin of…?
Are there any friends here?
Well, that didn't work! What next?
How can I maintain good relationships with… THIS team?
Should I really…?
What's next?
What now!?
I dislike the uncertainties of all these uncertainties.

> *One thing sure about missionary life is that it's full of uncertainties.*

Over my past thirty-plus years of missionary life and service, myriads of missionary uncertainties come to mind. Below are some of the uncertainties we recently received in answer to a question I posed to missionaries online: **What is your most certain uncertainty?**

Tim & Julie: Visa and immigration issues have been a significant uncertainty for us in missionary life. Over our 32 years of ministry, one constant has been that the immigration laws and policies of the world's 200+ countries are ever-changing.

As we enter month 11 of our visa process, we are reminded of the importance of faith and trust in the Lord's timing. We are confident that his timing is perfect, even if it means waiting a little longer to board a plane to our target country.

We just found out last week that the neighborhood of the city we plan to live is considered one of the worst for crime. That was the first time we had heard that. It doesn't change our plans for living there, but we now know that we will need to take additional precautions.

All this uncertainty carries practical consequences. Right now, we have suitcases and household belongings in 5 countries in various parts of the world.

It has been quite challenging to think through our next steps and how to pack and plan for them.

David: Our older parents health. This is one uncertainty that weighs heavily on me, particularly with my father, who suffers from dementia.

Alex: Trust…who can I trust? If a ministry is to thrive in a culture where trust has been undermined, trust seems almost impossible to build.

Paul: Not knowing which of the other missionaries I can trust.

James: After pouring my life into 'nationals' within this culture, I've seen that they cannot be trusted over and over again.

Lisa: Safety. I never feel safe because I'm always looking to go from "safe place to safe place," except does such a place exist?

Cindy: We don't know whether we'll be allowed back in the country where we've lived and served for over twenty years.

Jean: The uncertainties of our teenage children leaving home to attend college, work, or whatever.

Steve: In all honesty, after trying just about everything here, I still wonder, "Why am I even wasting my time?"

Gert: I've served as a __. __. __. missionary for almost thirty years now, and all of us over fifty-five received notices that we're all going to be laid off. All I know is missionary life. What am I going to do now?

Bud: Over my missionary career, a dozen men came to Christ who expressed a call to become pastors. One day, after so many lies, immorality, and theft, to name a few, I packed it up and returned home.

Of the twelve, ten were considerably younger than me, the ages of my sons. Now, as an older man, I've outlasted them all, most dying from the direct results of their sinful lifestyles.

My uncertainty looks back, asking, "Did I waste my life in that place."

Angie: What happens if we get cancer, typhoid, dengue fever, malaria, or something else? Without insurance, I don't know what we'll do.

Sue: We returned home for leave and moved in with my parents. However, no sooner had we arrived than my husband told me he was leaving me. He flew back to _____ and moved in with the house girl we hired to work in our home. What are the kids and I are going to do now?

Brain & Theresa: Our children are not adjusting well to this new culture. How can we help them transition into living here?

Chris & Shena: OK, we're finally here. Now what?

Paul & Katlyn: Our marriage is falling apart. Not that it was in that good of shape to begin with, but now we're not sure we'll make it.

Louise: My husband just died, making me a missionary widow.

Jamie: My mother is dying. The only thing I can do to provide the long-term care she needs is to resign and return home unemployed.

One thing about all these uncertainties is sure: lots of qualms will always exist in missionary life.

Practical ways exist to deal with uncertainties particular to each missionary, sending agency, and other considerations. It is often better to act rather than react to uncertainties by reflecting on considerations and possibilities. Example:

The are **3 A's** of Life Coaching

Applying these 3 A's to almost any situation can significantly increase your efficiency in dealing with uncertainties. Here's an example:

Agenda: *What is the most pressing issue I face?*

Example: How can we best travel from one church, meeting, or group of people to raise support?

Awareness: *What are my options?*

How wise is it to drive twelve hours on Saturday to get to the church I'll be present at the next day, Sunday? What other options are there?

Action Plan: *What I'll embark upon to address this issue.*

I'll arrive on Friday, giving the family and me a day to rest before presenting our field on Sunday morning.

God's Certainty in an Uncertain World

Above all, God, OUR Jehovah Jirah, must become our first consideration in the uncertainties of this life.

The Bible gives two absolute truths about God: his promise through Abraham and his oath.[30] Hebrews 6:18

His promise to us comes through the Abrahamic Covenant in Genesis Twelve:

The Promise

All the families on earth will be blessed through you.

Genesis 12:3b

So all who put their faith in Christ [share the same blessing] Abraham received because of his faith.

Galatians 3:9

Our faith in Jesus Christ grafts us into Abraham's lineage, making us receivers of God's promise—his rest. This blessing of promise is conferred upon us through the finished work of Christ.

The Oath

Our blessing through Abraham, purchased by Christ's sacrificial death, is guaranteed by God's oath to keep this promise.

So God has given both his promise and his oath. These two things are unchangeable because it is impossible for God to lie.

Therefore, we who have fled to him for refuge can have great confidence as we hold to the hope that lies before us.

This hope is a strong and trustworthy anchor for our souls. It leads us through the curtain into God's inner sanctuary. Jesus has already gone in there for us...

Hebrews 6:18b-20a

The result of this truth is something we can latch onto during times of uncertainty.

Once, I missed a bus trip to the Minnesota State Capitol in St. Paul. Every year, a day is earmarked for Fire Service Day at the capitol. Fighters wearing a Red Fire Service Day Shirt are allowed access to Minnesota representatives for discussing matters unique to the fire service. While volunteering in the Fire Service, I never missed a year, except for this one time.

That morning, minor, unexpected uncertainties hurdled obstacles at every turn. The bus had just pulled out of the parking lot as I arrived, making a right turn at the stop light, and was gone. Ticked, I drove back to my office at the church.

The next day, the fire chief informed me that the bus driver lost control on the icy roads, careening off I 35 and fishtailing the back left section of the bus into a large tree—the place and seat I sat in every year prior.

The seat crushed into itself when it collided with the tree, but firefighters in the front of the bus were also injured. My chief said, "Don if you've been sitting in that seat like you always do, I just don't know if you'd be here today."

Moving Forward: Sometimes, life's uncertainties redirect us toward a better path, a God-path. I love this verse from Proverbs 16:9:

"We can make our plans, but the <u>LORD</u> <u>determines</u> <u>our</u> <u>steps</u>."

The LORD keeps you from all harm
and watches over your life.

The LORD keeps watch over you as
you come and go, both now and forever.

Psalm 121:7-8

Exasperating
Apprehensions

APPREHENSION /ˌaprəˈhen(t)SH(ə)n/ - anxiety or fear that something bad or unpleasant will happen.[31]

I remember standing with Kathy and our then three little boys, looking out the window of the DFW airport terminal in Dallas, Texas. On the runway sat the jet that would begin our journey to South Africa for the first time.

A voice kept repeating itself in my head.

"Are you completely out of your mind?"

My mother's words kept ringing out as well, "You're taking big risks, moving your family over there."

Apprehension of a calling that took years to put into place began eroding.

Standing looking at the jet that day created an opportunity for anxiety to flood my mind. Three days later, in South Africa, all that evaporated. It was time to focus on the task at hand.

It reminded me of playing football in high school. As a running back, the day of the game brought apprehension and a nervous stomach. But the first time I took a hit, getting knocked to the other side of the field, that uneasiness waned as my focus turned to playing the game.

For first-time missionaries, trepidation can take hold, producing anxiety and panic.

Recently, a missionary couple called us from the field. As they entered their first week of service in a third-world country, panic and anxiety seized them both. Six weeks later, they resigned.

Hosts of apprehensions can assault us in missionary life. Like:

- Sending children off to college for the first time.
- Wishing to be closer to your grandchildren.
- Dealing with aging frail parents from thousands of miles away.
- Working with a team of missionaries you don't particularly like.
- Being given an assignment by your mission agency requiring you to move to another country.
- Having another donor drop their support when you're already under supported. Three dropped us just this month.
- Going through the arduous process of obtaining visas and other government documents.
- Continually searching for a place to live for the short time you're 'home' on furloughs.
- Lack of medications on the field.
- Health issues.
- Financial dilemmas.
- Political unrest in the country you're living in.
- Mental health struggles.
- Adjusting to new foods. My stomach is still a mess seventeen years after returning to the States from Africa.
- Hearing gunshots and bombs going off in the distance while lying in bed.
- Realizing that old age finally caught up with you, reducing your physical abilities and sapping your strength to do what you genuinely love.
- Vaccination requirements.
- Another 8-hour power outage in the freezing cold winter.

- Quarantines.
- The difference in it all.
- Do I still want to be here?
- What will happen if...?

Behind the smiles of many missionaries often lies a quiet voice whispering,

"Are you sure?"
"Really sure?"
"You really want to do this?"
"What if..."
"And then what?"
"Hum?"

Carpe Diem

Carpe Diem, often translated as 'Seize the Day,' literally means in the language that Horace, the Roman poet, wrote, '**Pluck the Day.**'[32]

What apprehensions plucks away at your days? Who's in charge of those life pluckers? Something always plucks away at our days. A day is never neutral or docile. Change constantly takes place between our ears and within our souls.

When we allow unease to murmur its anxieties into our spiritual ears, apprehensions snatch our joy and soundness of mind. Here's what I think. Everyone has a plucker or two in their life.

[And I am distracted] at the noise of the enemy, because of the oppression and threats of the wicked; for they would cast trouble upon me, and in wrath they persecute me.

Psalm 55:3 AMPC

Identify Your Pluckers

What pluckers lurk within you? What or who controls your attitude towards objects, situations, and others? Um…what about God? Rather than allowing those pluckers to seize your emotions, remove unease from your soul, 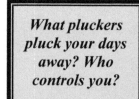 and replace it with something better. Grab hold of the day, squeezing every opportunity out of it. Move away from your:

> *What pluckers pluck your days away? Who controls you?*

Fear?
Anxiety?
Distrust?
Anger?
Worry?
Betrayal?

Plucker Quality Control — Philippians 4:6-7

1st Don't worry about <u>anything</u>;

2nd *Instead*, <u>pray</u> <u>about</u> <u>everything</u>.

- Tell God what you need,
- Thank him for all he has done.

3rd Then *experience* God's peace,

And then comes the great promise!

4th His ***peace*** *will **guard** your hearts and minds* as you <u>live in Christ Jesus</u>, which <u>exceeds anything we can understand.</u>

Then, you'll enjoy the benefits of the previous two verses;

Always be full of joy in the Lord. I say it again—<u>rejoice</u>! Let everyone see that you are considerate in all you do. **Remember, the Lord is coming soon.**

Philippians 4:4-5

Moving forward: What plucks at you throughout your day? If you can identify what causes your apprehensions, anxiety, fears, or whatever, you can act upon its angst, curtailing its effects before anxiety blooms in your soul.

Remember

Apprehension, anxiety, and worries are also part of the human experience. Trepidation grips most of us occasionally. However, chronic worry, apprehension, and anxiety are the enemy's most effective weapons, robbing us of our courage and joy.

We're most fortunate, however, because God promises to meet our every need, dismantling apprehension's pestering presence.

Because,

> ... this same God who takes care of me will supply all your needs from his glorious riches, which have been given to us in Christ Jesus.

Philippians 4:19

Commit everything you do to the Lord.
Trust him, and <u>he</u> <u>will</u> <u>help</u> <u>you</u>.

Psalm 37:5

Feared
Failures

Sometimes, perception becomes our reality,
whether based on fact or imagination.

FULL OF BLUSTER AND CONFIDENCE, the new missionary candidate stood with a group of soon-to-be-approved missionaries. He amplified the great work he'd start upon arriving on the field.

Throughout the week, his self-confidence commandeered many conversations in that group of candidates. Persistent observation tore open a verse in my soul.

> Pride goes before destruction,
> and haughtiness before a fall.[33]

Two years after arriving to the field, supporters and churches began receiving fewer updates. Then, no communication at all. Only questions surrounded this missionary's ghosting of everyone.

Finances waned as the young missionary panicked over the ever-decreasing resources 'to do the work of God.'

A few years later, he confessed, "Everything was going great! The facility we rented was superb to start a new church. We began seeing almost 100 people a week coming to my church. And…you know… in my country, well… now, that's really something."

Then, well, I don't know what happened! The numbers, the people, it all fell apart until, well, no one was coming. He shook his head in disgust.

I was ashamed and hid out, hoping people would just forget me.

I felt like God let me down.

I let God down.

He ended, "I couldn't bear it. All those people who put their trust in me. All the money they gave me. How could I ever look them in the eye again?"

So, he burrowed deep into obscurity, hoping people might forget him.

You know what? A compassionate group of believers surrounded that missionary. They loved and coached him back to health. Now, the work flourishes again on a much more solid footing. More importantly, the missionary is also thriving.

What was once perceived as a failure became a success story in many ways.

Long ago, we visited a missionary in their field of service, as we've done many times over the years. The day after our arrival, we sat at a table as the missionary began to share.

"When we went to the city of _____, God shut down my work. We returned to the States, worked in a church for a while, and then tried again in another field."

Looking down at the floor, he whimpered, "God's done it to me again."

After that, he changed fields of service a third time and resigned a year later. He blamed God for three ministry failures.

We don't handle losing well, do we? In our competitive sports cultures, winning is everything. Losing is a failure to win. Who remembers a second-place finisher?

Right?

We can measure the extent of our success by winning and losing. If it worked out the way I planned, it was a win! If not, it was a loss.

But not every failure is a loss. Failure can also produce wins.

Types of Failure

We can define 'failure' as a lack of success or the inability to meet an **expectation**.[34] Again, BACK TO EXPECTATIONS.

Failure is more than a social concept of not meeting a desirable or intended aim; it is usually viewed as the opposite of success.[35] There are different failures in missionary work, and my list is not comprehensive.

Unforeseen: that which we can't possibly know or expect. Many unanticipated situations arise, causing us to back up, retreat, and, hopefully, take a new look at the problem. I don't know how many missionaries grieve a perceived failure that is no fault of our own.

Sometimes we don't know what's out there. Often, what we think we know doesn't reflect reality.

Remember, "… we are not fighting against flesh-and-blood enemies, but against evil rulers and authorities of the unseen world, against mighty powers in this dark world, and against evil spirits in the heavenly places." Ephesians 6:12

Low Readiness: Failure can result from a lack of preparation. Missionaries heading out with great zeal, lacking training, mentoring, and expertise, floating on the tides of enthusiasm with extemporaneous attempts at 'doing a great work for God,' only to be dashed in perceived failure.

Complex Situations: Many intricacies and complexities arise beyond our ability to manage. We can take on more than we can handle to the detriment of everything else.

Sometimes, we need to ask, "Am I able to handle this? Do I possess the expertise for this venture?"

If not, build and manage a team for success. Some of the best missionaries I know build diverse teams. They accomplish this by bringing people into the team with better skill sets in areas they're weak, allowing them to cut through riptides of complexity, increasing the team's effectiveness.

Experimental Attempts: a new outreach, church plant, school, hospital, or approach that doesn't develop.

Some ministry launches prove unsuccessful. No sooner does it leave the launch into the jetties of possibilities that the effort capsizes, sinking once good intentions.

Like the 17th-century Swedish warship heralded as "the most spectacular warship ever built." With a burst of wind, the Vasa sank twenty minutes after it set sail, in full view of a horrified audience.[36]

Sometimes, our attempts sink as soon as they're launched. This is part of the journey. As my son regularly responds,

"Hey, it happens."

Don't flog yourself over a failed attempt. It is better to try but fail than to be one of the many who attempt nothing beyond what's comfortable.

Successful Failures: occur when lessons learned from failure produce a change in approach, viewpoint, or method which become a catalyst for success.

Reuters reported, "The spectacular explosion of SpaceX's new Starship rocket minutes after it soared off its launch pad on a first flight test is the latest vivid illustration of a 'successful failure' business formula that serves Elon Musk's company well."[37]

God-directed Failures: What about when God says, "Ah-ah, No" to our plans and efforts? It's always good to consider this possibility. Sometimes, a good idea is not a God idea.

A friend, pastoring what many might call an insignificant church, considered accepting the senior pastorship at a large church in Dallas. Just as he readied to accept the call, a Brown Recluse spider bit him on the toe.

The bite landed him in hospital, with his big toe eventually being amputated, in a yearlong recovery process.

He said, "I think that was God saying, 'ah-ah,' you stay put."

When prevented from preaching the word in the province of Asia, Paul headed for Bithynia, but God prevented entrance into that region as well.

What initially seemed like a setback turned into a divine redirection to Macedonia, Greece. There, Paul and Silas enjoyed numerous opportunities to share the Good News. A testament to the unexpected success that can follow apparent failure.

But they ended up in jail. Failure? No. This marked another God-directed opportunity to share in Jesus' suffering, giving witness to their Hope and Glory.

God and Failure

Sometimes, we base failure upon our view of God. How we understand God's person and validation of our efforts.

Within our ministries, churches, missionary callings, or whatever we want to call them, we've got to understand that it's all

> *Sometimes a 'failure' is divine redirection.*

about Christ, in Christ, and through Christ—Christ over our human perceptions of success.

61

After all, who is the cornerstone of the Church? Who died for the Church? What is the Church to proclaim? And what is the Gospel? Isn't it Jesus, plus nothing, minus nothing?

Everything was created through him and for him.

Colossian 1:16c

What's It All About Then?

It's not about you, me, or anyone other than God's ultimate consummation of the things to come through Jesus Christ.

Our God is in the heavens, and he does as he wishes.

Psalm 115:3

Finding the Win

Let's latch onto this often misquoted, taken out-of-context, misapplied verse in Romans 8:28.

God works everything together for the good. Ok…but we miss something here if we end it right there at verse twenty-eight.

What Good? This 'good' is often interpreted as 'what's best for me.' All the tough things in my life eventually work out for my benefit because God loves me.

That application places us, not God, at the center of this verse.

In verse twenty-nine, you'll find the phrase, *"he chose them to become like his Son…"*

The King James version uses the word 'conform.' To conform them—us—to the image of his Son.

God 'marked out beforehand' every event in our lives to conform us—to make us similar to his Son, Jesus Christ.

This considers the last part of verse 8:27, *"… in harmony with God's own will."*

62

Everything eventually agrees with His plans, not necessarily our perceptions or expectations of what that plan should look like.

In verse twenty-six, this working out for good, becoming more like Jesus, allows the Holy Spirit to help us in our weaknesses—i.e., failures—and assists us with our prayers *as the Holy Spirit prays for us with groanings that cannot be expressed in words*. Romans 8:26b

It works out then for our success?

Not necessarily.

Self-affirmation?

Well…

Self-esteem?

Ah…

So that I feel good about the results?

Not always.

It livens up my updates to supporters back home…

Hum…

To raise more funds?

Well, maybe, but…that better not be the direct object of your heart: money.

Sorry, but what we feel about something that does or doesn't work out isn't the primary consideration. Better questions to ask are:

What is God doing here?

How can I get involved?

Where will God receive glory above myself?

How will this make me more like Christ?

Instead of dwelling on what we consider success or failure, let's focus on how these experiences bring us closer to Jesus. The 'why' is often unanswerable anyway, leading to unnecessary angst. Perhaps, in the next life, the 'why' won't matter. So, let's not waste our time on it now. Instead, let's focus on our relationship with Jesus and how we can grow spiritually through our experiences.

I like Michael Kelly's words here:

1. God works for our good, not our comfort.
2. God works in all things, not just big things.
3. God works according to His purpose, not ours.[38]

The focal point of God's workings in our lives centers on one fundamental concept.

'And we know that God causes **everything to work together for the good** of those who love God..."

For God knew his people in advance, and he **chose them to become like his Son**... Romans 8:29

Make Us More Like Jesus

Does not this truth-changing perspective of success or failure resonate? Any event we might interpret as failure may bring us into harmony with God, molding us into some similarity with Christ.

Hey, from a human perspective, Jesus always had success. Really?

Let's pause and consider, from a human perspective, did Jesus always have success?

Like all those who abandoned him when he refused to do another miracle at their bidding.

His closest friends who couldn't even stay awake to pray with him.

A denouncing Peter.

A lying, thieving, betraying Judas.

The 'assembly' of those Jewish Religious leaders of the day, filled with envy and fear, who tried to kill Jesus and eventually succeeded.

When no one came to help him during his last hours on the Cross, how did Jesus respond to these supposed failures? He assigned every result to the Father.

Success or failure allocates the results to God rather than how we might think or interpret them.

'My thoughts are nothing like your thoughts,' says the Lord. 'And my ways are far beyond anything you could imagine.

For just as the heavens are higher than the earth, so my ways are higher than your ways and my thoughts higher than your thoughts.'

Isaiah 55:8-9

My friends, this relationship we're in and the work we're doing may have less to do about us and everything to do with God.

It's not about you.
It's not about me.
Or that mega-church pastor.
The Christian author of all those books.
That missionary's dozens of works compared to others' few.
How many people you have in your church.
The amount of financial support you do or don't have.
What others do or don't think about…
How busy you are.

How **big** or small your ministry is.

65

It's about God's glory and declaring it so.

How do we mark success or failure? Failure can succeed if it leads to a rethinking and relaunching of an effort towards a better result.

God does whatever God does. God doesn't answer to you, me, or anyone else, regardless of whether we interpret life events as successes, failures, or whatever.

What God does do is hear our prayers, answering them according to his will and the purity of our requests.

Who says a church, school, or hospital that closed is a failure?

Who says an organization with all those people and money is successful?

That's God's business, and we'll know about that standing before Him if we hear, "*Well done*, my good and faithful servant." Matthew 25:21

WE STARTED FOUR CHURCHES and a care center for women and children in South Africa. Two of those church buildings no longer exist after the members disbanded.

Who's failure is that?

Is it a failure?

Is it a 3 to 2 score in favor of success? This marks a .600 success rate which is pretty good.

Right?

But is this the measure of success…or failure? After all, every church mentioned in the New Testament no longer exists. Where are the churches of Laodicea, Philadelphia, Corinth, Antioch, or Jerusalem? That's not to say God's people are not represented there today.

I occasionally receive communication from Zulu adults who were children in our ministry many years ago. They love Jesus and share that love with others, buildings or no buildings.

What 'failure' hides behind your smile, hovering over you with words like,

Give up.

You're no good at this.

Cover it with a smile.

What's the purpose of it anyway?

When looking through failure's eyes, go easy on yourself because "... God, who began the good work within you, will continue his work until it is finally finished on the day when Christ Jesus returns." Phil 1:6

Remember

We all fail someone, somewhere, or at something at one time or another. Failure is part of being human. It may aid us in becoming better, more aware, and wiser about our next ventures.

Lack of success can run us aground or...push us to patch our sails, repair the masks, and catch the winds of accomplishment. No one has ever arrived at success without a series of failures, and history fills pages with such accounts.

Let failure become your steppingstones, moving you forward to the prize in Christ Jesus.

> "Failures are finger posts on the road
> to achievement."[41]
>
> — C.S. Lewis

My health may fail, and my spirit may grow weak,
but God remains the strength of my heart;
he is mine forever.

Psalm 73:26

Sporadic
Scarcities

WE'D BECOME GOOD FRIENDS. Paul met Jackie, an Irish lass, during a YWAM rally in Durban, South Africa. After a short courtship, they married.

Paul, a South African, had already served as a missionary, predominantly among the Zulu people. Soon, after Jackie's approval by Paul's missions agency, she became a certified missionary as well.

They worked in Dundee, Natal, just an hour from Kathy and me. We enjoyed many hours together, sharing both the merits and challenges of missionary life.

After they returned from visiting Jackie's family in Belfast, Ireland, we sat down for coffee together at a local Wimpy's restaurant. Paul made a U-turn in the conversation.

"You know, Don, it throttled me when visiting family and friends in Ireland to see how much everyone has."

The phrasing of Paul's words garnered my attention.

"I am not complaining," he continued. "But it floored us to see how we faired compared to our friends. They live in delightful houses and drive expensive vehicles. I mean, we'll never see anything like that, ever. We've spent the best-earning years of our 30s and 40s here in South Africa doing missionary work. We'll never earn enough to live like that."

Jackie added, "Missionary life means sometimes going without."

I could instantly relate. Over the years, we'd returned for furloughs in the United States, traveling all over the country and reporting to supporters. Kathy mentioned several times, "Whenever we're in someone's nice, fancy home, you get very quiet."

 A lingering thought accompanied my smile, "We'll never live in anything that nice, find furniture like that, or live anywhere safe. And...I'll never drive an F150 like my friend. It sets me back, I guess. What really stands out are the huge flat-screen TVs everyone has."

Of course, my smile constantly communicated, "We're trusting God and are completely content."

But I love F150 pickups! Somehow, my South African 2.4-liter 4-cylinder Toyota 5-speed Hilux 4x4, without air conditioning or power steering, didn't quite cut it any longer compared to my brother's truck in Minnesota.

I know; I Know... be satisfied with what you've got. Right? RIGHT?

AND shame on you, you're a missionary. Missionaries should never want all that stuff anyway. After all, we're super spiritual, not suffering such vices." Huh?

Let's be honest. Behind the smiles we present to supporters back home, an epic struggle about our station in life can exist.

So, let's talk about it. OK? I'm not criticizing any missionary's actions here. Still, I want us to gain a healthier, Scripture-focused, God-centered view of the cost of our missionary callings—a calling that I've struggled with at times when measuring up against my counterparts.

This life we live demands sacrifice. That's just the way it is. I've handled far more money than most of my family, friends, and supporters will ever see while earning far less than any of them.

I've been cautious in handling development funds raised over the years. Our largest project was over $250,000. Yet, my personal bank account never reflected those amounts.

Going without is a part of it all—it is sort of an abdication of wanting the stuff many Christians sitting in churches back home possess.

Yet...

Upon leaving South Africa and returning to Minnesota, my birthplace, thoughts centered on, "I've done my time! I want the American Dream like everyone else."

A nice boat.

Hunting rifles.

An F150 truck.

High-quality furniture.

New high-end fishing gear.

And MY OWN HOUSE!

The church I pastored helped us build a delightful house in the woods of northern Minnesota. I loved those people and that place: the house, the four-season porch, the woods, the wildlife...I'd finally arrived.

I bought a nice used boat with a live well, a trolling motor, and everything else I wanted.

Bought me an F150 pickup truck, too.

And... a nice big, I mean huge, flat-screen plasma TV, which was the thing in those days.

I settled, or so I thought.

You know what?

I'd been lucky to pay that house off by the time I reached seventy. Everyone that made that area special to me, grandparents, parents, aunties, and uncles, were gone long ago.

And that plasma flat screen T.V.? It was out of fad within a year or two after I bought it.

All those things I wanted and got didn't fill any vacuum left upon leaving missionary service. Besides, what do we ever possess? Everything we have is given to us and gone with our last breath.

Since being diagnosed with Facioscapulohumeral Muscular Dystrophy, I've given most of that stuff away as I'm no longer physically able to use it. Puts things into perspective.

Investing in the Gospel pays far better dividends. Jesus reminds us that sacrifices may seem high now, but the result is well worth our sacrifices and expenditures. Peter grumbled, "We've given up everything to follow you."

> *Investing in the Gospel pays far better dividends.*

Really, Peter, a lot, but everything? Have you ever felt that way?

Like, "God, do you know how much I've gone without to be a missionary? No one appreciates me for that!" I love Jesus' reassuring response to Peter:

> I assure you that **everyone who has given up** house or brothers or sisters or mother or father or children or property, **for my sake** and for the Good News, **will receive now in return a hundred times** as many houses, brothers, sisters, mothers, children, and property... Mark 10:29b-30a

One hundred times more, hum… pretty good investment, huh?

Where's your pleasure? What metric do we use to find value? You know, we concern ourselves with many things. Not that they're unimportant—of course they are—but compared to the heavenly, not so much.

An intimate relationship with the Lord of Creation, The Great I Am, is intrinsically more valuable. When God becomes our primary focus, our desires align with His, and we can find joy in the things of this world without losing sight of Him.

> Seek the Kingdom of God above all else, and live righteously, and he will give you everything you need.
>
> Matthew 6:33

> Take delight in the Lord, and he will give you your heart's desires.
>
> Psalm 37:4

When God began pricking my attention towards missionary care, the hardest thing I've ever done was leave the very place I dreamed about living.

Upon returning to Northern Minnesota, my thoughts centered around:

I need a place to live.

I need a church to attend and serve.

I need a place to die.

I need a place to be buried.

I had it all figured out.

As we drove out of town after selling our house, the love gift given to us by so many good people in our church, a house I loved, and having also sold our nice furniture for almost nothing, Kathy said, "Whew, getting rid of all that stuff is very freeing."

Kathy's often ahead of me on faith's trail.

Now, we are on the other end of that decision: living in someone else's house rent-free and on a lake, which has been a lifelong dream.

And guess what? Churches helped us purchase very nice F150!

Now, we come alongside hundreds in missionary member care. Something that God prepared us for through much pain. That continues to this day.

Yet, even on my worst days—and I have them—let me tell you, His provisions constantly amaze, reassuring us of his watchful care over us.

 Yesterday, on the phone with our son Dan, he said, "You know, Dad, God has never abandoned you yet. I've been amazed at how God seemingly takes care of you and Mom out of nowhere."

Upon leaving the American pastorate, I discovered that what I missed most from missionary life was *living on faith's edge* and trusting God in every circumstance for just about everything.

God's miraculous provision through His people, something we couldn't network on our best day, continually reminds us of the amazing lifestyle and calling we now live.

As my last chapters of life approach, I'm learning to be content. There's nothing I'd rather be doing than what I'm doing right now. Keeping our eyes on the prize.

Part of the missionary experience is going without. But God replaces our 'withouts' with more satisfying provisions. And...going without is small compared to the immense sacrifice of our Savior hanging on that old cross in agony, paying the price, atoning for our sins.

And everyone who has given up houses or brothers
or sisters or father or mother
or children or property, for my sake, **will receive a
hundred times as much in return**
and will inherit eternal life.

Matthew 19:29

Unintentional
Entitlements

BY THE SAME TOKEN, as we experience deprivations, disregard, and sometimes disrespect, we can gradually unknowingly allow an attitude of missionary entitlement to overtake us.

We inherit mission systems of fundraising, approval processes, personal relations, promotion, and so on. Support-raising missionaries find themselves in faith arenas, living off the gifts of others.

This is not bad, but it lends itself to an inherent snare; unintentional entitlement attitudes. *A feeling or belief that we intrinsically deserve privilege or special treatment* [40] *simply because we're missionaries.*

Missionaries fraught with attitudes of privilege probably didn't start their missionary careers with this deficit. However, the system does lend itself to greed and demand.

> We must become acutely aware of the developing
> an entitlement attitude.

Most churches give us love offerings when we present our call to missions. We're put up in decent motels, well... most of the time, anyway. They cover our meals and sometimes spoil our children, giving us tickets to Disney World and other attractions.

During my missionary career, pastors have taken my son's skeet shooting, fishing, hiking, and a host of other kindnesses offered.

And... often, people regard us with some reverence because of our willingness to go where we're going to go and do what we're going to do.

We depend upon these churches and people. However, an 'I deserve' attitude can become a silent mantra.

"Because I'm a missionary, giving up so much, you should... for me..."

The Subtle Encroachment of Entitlement

During a gathering of pastors, a missionary approached me, assailing, "I've emailed you, left you a voice mail, and texted you, but you've not responded. What a SHAME!" The accosting grabbed the attention of several other pastors in the room.

I don't know; perhaps it's a weakness, but my first defense is to shut down when someone does that to me. I walk away, ignore, and marginalize.

As I've gotten older, that kind of hostility receives little of my time. So, as a large church pastor at that time, I walked away without acknowledging the missionary.

Later, he sat down uninvited at lunch beside me, firing verbal piercings again. With pastors sitting around us, I responded differently this time as he tried to guilt-trip me.

A voice whispered in my head, "Ok, you want a fight; you got it, pal!" Have I ever told you I get grumpy at times?

So, I landed a stiff verbal counter-punch, "Hold it a minute. First, who are you?"

Well, I'm a missionary.

"Oh, does our church support you?"

Wait, you mean you don't even know who your church supports?

"Okay, that's a nice try at pejorative condensation, but I don't know all the missionaries my church supports."

Now, I was ready for battle. Putting up my guard, I landed a couple jabs.

"I've just started pastoring there, and since we give over 200,000 dollars a year spread out to over 150 missionaries, 6 Christian organizations, and a host of special missionary projects each year, I've not gone down the list of missionaries we support and memorized it yet."

Then, the uppercut, "A list, by the way, you'll most likely never be on."

I told you; I can get gnarly sometimes.

Immediately, "I'm sorry, pastor, I think I've overstepped."

With my mood calming down, "Look, my friend, I know support and fundraising are difficult. I was a missionary, too."

"You need to understand, however, that I can't respond to every missionary. As this is the first American church I've pastored, the demands overwhelm me a bit."

I went on, "Most of these pastors here today possess little margin of time even to take care of themselves and their families. Many of us in this room have also been yelled at by some moody, disrespectful church member this week."

I lowered my tone, "The response you want comes through our missions team. They review all the requests and recommend candidates to our elders. Because we support so many already, they only bring in one or two new candidates a year. They've decided not to invite you if you haven't heard from them."

My message was correct, but I probably threw an uppercut or two too many. Well, maybe. Who knows? Yet several pastors appreciated the frank response that, as one said, "I wish I dared to do so."

Just last week, after kicking off a Missions Emphasis Month for a church only forty minutes from us, we packed up, went to lunch, which the church paid for, and then, with goodbyes, returned home.

Ten minutes into the ride, I remarked to Kathy, "Hum...they didn't give us an honorarium," or, as we call it in our circles, a love offering. We had to cover our own expenses.

Then I got the look. You know what the look is. Don't you?

A facial communique from someone close to you, in my case Kathy, that said, "It's not a problem. Let it go."

Right?

Even though it's customary in our circles to give missionaries love offerings, it's not owed. And though it's come to be anticipated, it shouldn't be expected.

The next time I bumped into that pastor at a meeting, I smiled and greeted him, all the while thinking, "You stiffed us."

And again, we return to the idol of expectation—*this is what I deserve, what I want, and what you owe me because...*

 Only a week later, at another missions conference, a gentleman approached me and gave me a folded check. That evening, I was looking at a thousand-dollar gift. Then, at the end of the conference, a huge celebration followed. There, the same individual sat down next to me.

He slid another folded check in front of me. I thanked him as we continued talking.

Guess what? Towards the end of our conversation, he slid me a third folded check!

No joke, I'm not making this up.

As he got up to leave, I said, "Wait! Don't leave yet."

He replied, "We have more to talk about?"

Grinning, I responded, "Oh, I figured if I could keep you here another twenty minutes, I'd get another check out of you." We both roared with laughter.

That night, we received two more checks, each worth $1,000, totaling $3,000 for the week. This exceeded our expenditures from the previous week, during which we received no financial remuneration. Our expenses for the month were more than covered.

That's a God-thing!

Missionary Entitlement: It's there. We fall for it all the time. There is an assumption that special privileges, allowances, and considerations are owed because of the uniqueness of the missionary calling, the lack of missionaries on the field, and the exclusivity of missionary work.

Yes, we rely on churches' crucial support to meet our financial needs, and they will, and they do.

We possess unique God-callings requiring a gamut of resources and opportunities. They'll come.

Missionaries need vehicles, funds for shipping, setting up homes in new countries, funds for special projects, considerations for their children and friends, and much more.

> *You'll __always__ have everything you __need__.*

And God will generously provide all you need. Then you will always have everything you need and plenty left over to share with others.

2 Corinthians 9:8

Let's Remember:

- No one owes me anything except God, who promises to provide for my needs.

80

- I requested the opportunity to present, so I'm a guest. Guests don't assume or demand.

- A polite, well-thought-out request is not a demand.

- Focusing on assumptions objectifies people as mere suppliers of what I want, placing me in the center of my wants.

- Any consideration, kindness, or gift, regardless of the size, is more than I deserve.

- My only response can be one of gratitude and joy.

- Become as good a giver as you are a receiver.

- Try giving your love offering to another struggling missionary just starting out.

I know a well-supported missionary woman in her seventies who regularly buys struggling missionaries plane tickets for their travel.

Upon returning home from their fields of service, others gave their vehicles to missionaries rather than selling them.

This missionary has paid for many pastor's lunches, asking the server to bring the ticket to me.

Rather than sell our furniture when we left South Africa, we gave much of it away to missionaries.

 Moving Forward: A murdered veteran missionary woman in her seventies, killed on the field in her own home, left instructions in her will. After the funeral, her son called our missions director, explaining that his frugal mother asked him to invest most of her modest monthly support, starting a fund to help missionaries ship their goods to the field upon their first arrival. The amount she left to our missions agency astounded us.

Remember: Entitlement drives us to a false Eden[41] rather than resting in God's provision. Entitlement becomes tainted fruit, depriving us entrance into our gardens, which is God's best for our lives.

42

Give your burdens to the LORD,
and he will take care of you.
He will not permit the godly to slip and fall.

Psalm 55:22

Baffling
Betrayals

WHEN WE LEFT FOR THE FIELD, our church promised to help us buy all the things we needed once we arrived.

Our pastor promised, "As soon as you get to the field and figure out what you need, where you'll get it, and how much it will cost, we'll deposit the money in your account."

Within three weeks of arriving, they submitted a thorough, well-thought-out list of required items and the cost.

No reply.

Finally, when they called their 'Home Church,' an office assistant said, "Pastor resigned last week."

Can you imagine?

The couple went into a muffled panic.

No, kidding...who wouldn't?

After speaking with the Head Deacon, a church leadership meeting followed. A week later, that deacon informed them that no one in leadership knew anything about an arrangement.

"I'm sorry about all of this. We were totally in the dark. And...well... the church doesn't have nearly enough money right now to help you meet all your needs."

Has anyone ever handed you a lollapalooza like that?

Of course, it devastated the couple. The betrayal threatened to eat them up.

However, they hung in there as the church took up special offerings to help supply some of their needs.

They refused to become angry and bitter.

Today, you'll find them faithfully serving twenty-plus years in their field of God's calling.

Now, I wish all missionaries weathered such storms similarly, but many do not.

Recently, a missionary used the phrase 'ultimate betrayal' to describe their feelings towards their Sending Church.

Usually desiring to unravel an issue, I replied, "How were you betrayed?"

Betrayal: the sense of being harmed by the *intentional* actions or *omissions* of a trusted person.[43]

Unintentional Omissions

Was the betrayal an omission, a slip-up, miscommunication, an error in judgment, a misunderstanding of what was said, or something that elapsed over a long period and was forgotten?

A few times over the years, more than a donor or two forgot to follow up on something they'd promised us. Upon enquiring, most couldn't recall the conversation.

Life is busy. Words many. Memories short. In this, omissions occur all the time. We're fallible human beings bombarded with information overloads daily.

People have told me, "But you said that…"

We've all been there, haven't we?

My thoughts often hover around:

I did?

When?

Where?

People forget. I've learned to cut others a lot of slack for simply not recalling a conversation.

> *Misunderstandings that appear as betrayals are often omissions of unintentional consequences.*

Missionary...sometimes anger takes hold, turning into negative emotions over a mere oversight.

We must develop a discipline of overlooking errors by omission and the unintentional consequences of previous conversations and actions.

Make allowance for each other's faults, and forgive anyone who offends you. Remember, the Lord forgave you, so <u>you</u> <u>must</u> <u>forgive</u> others.

Colossians 3:13

Has anyone ever asked you to forgive for an 'offense,' but you couldn't remember any of it?

Similarly, have you ever found yourself in a situation where someone is accusing you of something you can't recall? No matter how hard you try, the incident remains a blank, yet the accuser is standing right in front of you, insisting:

You did...

You said...

You meant... — To Me

You promised...

Response, "Hey, sorry, I don't recall such a conversation."

Yet, there's that person with a solidified mind like hardened concrete yapping, "You offended me."

Pops, we called him in Bible College. He once asked me to forgive him for an offense he felt he'd committed against me. For the life of me, I couldn't recall any offense.

"Will you forgive me?" he asked.
Well, pops, what was the offense?
"I'm not going to tell you," he replied.
Well, I will not forgive you then.
We both broke out in laughter.

Question: is it possible, no matter how infinitesimally improbable, that you just forgot about an encounter or misconstrued a conversation?

Apologies: If someone accuses me of offending them and it's beyond my recall, I'll always apologize for the possibility that something happened.

"My friend, hey…sorry, I don't remember that conversation or incident. All I can do to make this right is to ask you for a little grace and overlook the issue. Can you do that?"

Now, I'll usually express regret for misunderstandings… but I'll only ask for forgiveness if I'm culpable. I'm not in the habit of offering forgiveness to appease someone for their deluded thinking of an event when I know that such and such never happened.

Ever have a person so upset with you they almost accuse of a crime over nothing? They fabricate a story, believing firmly that an occurrence happened when it did not.

We have a saying in Northern Minnesota:

It's not what you know that you don't know that gets you into trouble; rather, what you don't know that you know that causes most difficulties.

86

Sometimes, people hold an indefensible position behind false accusations, a made-up story, mistaken identity, flawed memory, or just plain stupid stubbornness. You can't win with that kind of person. So, acknowledging a nonculpable accusation simply to appease someone over a misinterpretation of recalling an event amounts to dishonest pragmatism.

It's a lie of agreement to pacify a problematic person.

Here, I'll hold my ground, starting with gentle words and working towards a crescendo of a solid response.

"I don't recall such a thing."

"From my viewpoint, that's not accurate."

"I don't see it that way."

"Perhaps you're mistaken about that."

"Well, it looks like we can't resolve this, so I'm going to let it go."

Grace Principle: Extend the same grace to others you wish others might extend to you.

Often, an offense comes from negative emotions caused by a word or an action that <u>conflicts with what we expect and believe to be right</u>, appropriate, moral, and acceptable behavior.[44]

Learn to overlook perceived offenses, or they'll eat you alive. People rarely act according to my or your sense of right and wrong. This includes Christians.

Sometimes, perceived offenses amount to nothing more than a failure to meet hopeful assumptions of a conversation, meeting, or correspondence. That'll often result in confusion, disappointment, and convoluted relationships.

> *If you want grace, you've got to extend grace.*

87

Intentional Offenses

Was the betrayal a deliberate act to harm, dishearten, or defeat, with the intent of wounding a person? There's a massive difference between omission and intention. If deliberate…

Forgive: I <u>regret</u> <u>doing</u> it. Forgive me for causing you… Forgive me for what I did to you….

How can I make this right?

Here, I'm admitting to an offense and seeking forgiveness and reconciliation.

Forgiveness is not forbearance, overlooking, or putting up with… In seeking forgiveness, I'm asking another to dismiss my offense, not count it against me, and reconcile with me to a restored functional relationship.

Is this not what God does for us through his Son, Jesus Christ? Outside of a relationship with Christ we stand apart from God.

> If you forgive those who sin against you, your heavenly Father will forgive you. <u>But</u> <u>if</u> <u>you</u> <u>refuse</u> to forgive others, your Father <u>will</u> <u>not</u> <u>forgive</u> <u>your</u> <u>sins</u>.
>
> —Jesus Matthew 6:14

Jesus said, *if you don't forgive, you won't be forgiven.* I'm not obligated to merge Christ's words with theological arguments. We do, however, need to heed Jesus instruction:

If you want forgiveness you've got to forgive.

 Behind our smiles often lies unforgiveness, eating away at our souls. What's the struggle? What's keeping you from perfecting the Art of Forgiveness—releasing someone from an offense? What…?

88

If you want forgiveness, you must forgive. Once, a missionary commented to me, "If so-and-so—another missionary—dropped dead right now. I'd be okay with that." What?

Only in forgiveness can we live the love of Jesus Christ. **Who do you need to forgive?** Live free in forgiveness or shackled in bitterness and disregard. It's a choice…

> Be kind, for everyone you meet is fighting a battle you know nothing about.
>
> Wendy Mass

LORD, if you kept a record of our sins, who,
O Lord, could ever survive? But you
offer forgiveness, that we might learn to fear you.

Psalm 130:3-4

Disheartening Disappointments

"Disappointment and failure aren't identical,
they often occur together, and both can hold us back
from God's best for our lives."

— Billy Graham

BEHIND MANY A MISSIONARY'S SMILE can lay a series of disappointments unique to the missionary lifestyle. Sometimes these disappointments consume us.

Our disenchantments may appear unnoticed at first, like the vast iceberg that sank the Titanic, ninety percent of the glacier hid below the icy waters of the North Atlantic unnoticed until striking it.[45]

Icebergs of Disappointments

How about the missionary couple that their church recalled from the field? Upon arriving home, leadership informed them, "We sent the _____'s to take over the work. You'll need to find somewhere else to go." True story.

That faithful couple was replaced by staff members from their Home Church, taking over a multimillion-dollar ministry.

Arriving in Asia, the people rejected the unannounced strangers who didn't understand the culture or speak their language.

Tentacles of damage affected financial donors; supporting the work through that missionary couple. They ceased their donations.

Twenty years of work ended in crashing waves of deception, betrayal, and disappointment. Was it any wonder they chucked it and left the ministry afterward?

They left the field, left the church, and left the faith.

Those icebergs of:

- You've got thirty days to leave the country.
- Your visas will not be renewed.
- A message while you're sitting in Somewhere, Wherever, that your dad just died.
- Your son, who is in college in Florida, was just admitted to hospital and is in the ICU near death.
- The pastor of your Home Church, in an extra-marital affair, resigns. When you hear about it, your once beloved church split with its members scurrying out the doors.
- Now, what's going to happen?
- The native leadership you've spent years training disintegrates.
- Your largest financial contributor stops supporting you.
- The vision that propelled you to raise all that money, move to another country, and learn a language...well, that's not quite working out.
- Continual health struggles because of living where you live.
- Dismay that after serving in Central America in a successful twenty-five-year ministry, a new director of your mission agency assigned you to a field change. They don't speak Spanish in Amsterdam, and you don't speak Dutch either. But hey, how hard will it be to learn another language at fifty-eight?
- Notification that because of dwindling returns within your denomination's Missions Trust Fund, you've got two years to find something else to do. Really happened.

Well, **"Suck it up."**

"Missionaries need to get tough!"

Or, my favorite, "Don, the mission field is not for sissies. Pull your socks up. Get back at it!"

How about, "Missionaries today don't love God as much because they're not as committed as they used to be."

Amidst the rationale and conversation, it's the results that concern me most.

One by one, disappointed souls, WIA—Wounded in Action— disappear from service and the church.

Bergy Bits and Growlers

Missionary disappointments often come in disheartening swells of disenchantments one upon another that can wash away our joy. I liken this to Bergy Bits and Growlers.

'Bergy bits' comprise smaller pieces of ice floating on the ocean's surface around 16 feet / 5 meters. Smaller still, ice less than 3 feet / 1 meter makes up 'growlers.'[46]

To me, bergy bits and growlers do the most damage, ending good intentions prematurely. The little things... King Solomon reminds us;

> Catch all the foxes, those little foxes, before they ruin the vineyard ...
>
> Song of Solomon 2:15

Like:

- Upon your arrival to the field, you must figure out how to connect your utilities, get hooked up to the internet, and get a phone connected. It took me over a year.
- A message received that another supporter dropped their financial support, making up a substantial part of your budget.
- Constant noise in the streets around your house.
- A gnawing feeling that you'll never get married.
- A calling that seemingly turns into a culling.

- The lament of knowing you'll probably never get a handle on the language.[47]
- Missionary friends exiting the field, leaving you alone.
- Returning home for a break after two years on the field where nobody even knew you were gone.
- When conflict becomes constant.
- Navigating a culture that seems impossible.
- Christmas on the field without family.
- The umpteenth time someone steals from you.
- Another one of your vehicles gone again.
- Blahs that leave you wanting to do nothing, so…you spend your time at the movie theaters, malls, or in bed pigging out on junk food and binge-watching shows.
- That niggling thought of "maybe, we'd, I'd, be better off back…"

After my TBI—traumatic brain injury—while struggling to regain speech without stuttering, a pastor said, "Get it together man! Ministry is tough everywhere."

This from an office where $30,000 of furniture adorned that rough ministry environment. Shortly after, the pastor went to lunch in his new luxury BMW.

That one encounter pulled a curtain of despondency over me. With that, we limped back to the field for our next term of service.

We now enjoy friendships of several compassionate, accessible pastors. We're thankful.

Slow Seepage

Once, I took a friend's ski boat to Spioenkop Dam, just thirty minutes from our home in Ladysmith, South Africa, for a day out with the family. Launching the boat into the water, our sons put their tubes in, ready for biscuiting around the dam. Then, I hit it.

93

Flying down the dam, rhinos drank from the shoreline. It took about thirty minutes to reach the other end. I turned the boat around to head back towards our picnic area. But the speed decreased dramatically as the Four-stroke 175 Hp Mercury engine started groaning, trying to make its way through the water.

We double-checked everything, including the boat drain plug. Everything seemed in order. Then, I noticed the boat's stern sitting low in the water.

So, we rechecked. You know what? Two boat plugs existed, one in the stern and another in the bow. A tethered bow drain plug sat unplugged below the deck as water seeped into the boat, forcing air through the flooring seams, producing a hissing sound.

Upon inserting the bow drain plug, we crawled back to the launch. Now laden with water in its hull, the boat's weight required us to drag it back onto the trailer.

We pulled both drain plugs as water poured out of the boat before snickering experienced boaters nearby.

Sometimes, slow, seeping disappointments can creep up and grind the life out of us.

Ever meet a crabby, grumpy, ill-tempered missionary? I know a missionary just like that. Sometimes, I look at him in the mirror. Of course, that's not the person I present when standing before audiences. No...there stands a confident, on-top-of-it-all person.

But twenty years in Africa, a head injury, and ineffective re-entry into American life—Muscular Dystrophy plus, plus, plus... tries to sink my once spunky, energetic disposition.

And I've had to deal with my perceived perspective of God for allowing all this stuff in my life as well.

Have you ever felt like God has betrayed you?

Turned his back on you?

Let you down?

Or just doesn't seem to care?

Like the missionary family, who was assured of housing upon their first arrival to the field. They stood in the airport waiting for a missionary to meet them and take them to their newly promised residence, but the missionary never arrived.

Neither did that house ever appear as well.

The missionary put his family in an airport hotel for the first two weeks. Three months later, he returned home with his family, to the bewilderment of many of their supporters.

They'd sold their home in the States before leaving for the field to dedicate themselves fully to the work. Now, they stood homeless, looking at the house they once owned.

His previous employer hired a replacement; he was jobless, too.

Now, you'll find a crabby guy trying to make a living for his family in a tiny house with a thirty-year mortgage over twice the monthly payment he made before leaving for the field. What a travesty.

But such dirty deals await any servant of God serious about entering the Gospel trenches of missionary service. It's the enemy's primary tool to disenfranchise us from our callings.

Navigating Disappointments

Disappointments often seem to organize in small waves, building upon each other like a series of ebbs and flows crashing upon us, pushing us way from our Savior.

How we handle our disappointments determines outcomes. Here are a few thoughts.

Find your people. Jennie Allen has written a fine book entitled *Finding Your People.* My takeaway from the book is to find people who can relate to your experiences. This is a principle of association.

Teachers talk with teachers.
Friends talk with friends.
Pastors talk with pastors.
Children on the playground find other children to play with.
Lawyers converse with other lawyers on legal matters.
Firefighters talk with firefighters.
Businesspeople interact with each other.
Friends interact with friends.

So, then, Missionaries talk with…. Whom?

Find your people, missionary. Sometimes, other missionaries who've hung in there and overcome obstacles may become colleagues in relating to our struggles.

What's their secret?
How do they overcome?
What did it take to acquire the language?
Where can I find…?

Get around some positive, motivated people. I intentionally developed friendships with successful businesspeople during my years in South Africa.

No, we didn't discuss ministry. Instead, effective people in other fields offered intravenous drips of encouragement. Professionals at the top of their game provided renewed motivation because conversations focused on their successes rather than my discontents.

Motivated, optimistic problem solvers, forward-moving, thinking businesspeople, inspired a get-up-and-get-at-it-again attitude.

I remember Jeff telling me about one of his financial endeavors going belly up.

What are you going to do, Jeff?

He replied, "Ah…it's not the first time one of my businesses went under. We'll give it another shot tomorrow."

What happens if you lose it all?

"Well, it wouldn't be the first time."

How do you recover from this?

"I'll look back at how I might have done things differently—a smarter, more efficient way to accomplish things for future endeavors."

> *Get around some positive motivated people.*

That was in the same week someone pinched his car, and a tremendous storm in the Indian Ocean wrecked and sank his catamaran docked in a port in Durban, South Africa.

Quite a different attitude from some of the whining, complaining, life-is-so-hard missionaries I've met. Relax. I'm also referring to some of my past attitudes, too. OK?

How about chalking up your disappointments towards a learning curve you'd gain nowhere else. What are its most outstanding lessons? Maybe write them down here:

1. _____

2. _____

3. _____

Then a take-charge approach, "What I will not repeat that resulted in that kerfuffle?"

Don't allow disappointments to fester. Often, a tiny problem swells in into gales because we dwell and fixate upon it.

I went to an optometrist yesterday about my running, seeping, gooey left eye—a problem I had put off for two months. After the doctor examined me, he said, "Well, it can't be that simple, can it?" "I like simple!" announcing back.

All my trouble in that eye stemmed from a lower ingrown eyebrow that lay inside next to the lacrimal gland. The next day, after the eyebrow was removed, there was no more seeping and oozing.

I can't count the number of missionaries who couldn't get over an altercation with another organization, church, or person. An unforgiving goop oozed from their souls.

You've got to let discontents go. Otherwise, they become infected, growing into gangrenous implications.

Learn to cope with your disappointments. Paying attention to disappointment's reactions may become very helpful.

When that happened, I... Write it down. Dare yah.

> _____

> _____

> _____

As well, too...What led up to that letdown that's so difficult for me to overcome?

> _____

> _____

> _____

Take another shot! Understand that disappointment is a part of life, something we all experience. You don't want to be that person who sits on the bench, refusing to play the game, do you?

If a baseball player retires with an ERA (Earned Run Average) of .400, they become part of an elite group. On September 28, 1941, Ted Williams got 6 hits in 8 at-bats during the last game of the season to become the last player to retire from Major League Baseball with an above—400 batting average.[48]

Tony Gwyn came closest in 1994 when he finished 3 hits shy of .400 during a strike-shortened season and ended the season with a .394 ERA.[49]

Over eighty years have passed, and no player in the majors has reached that mark since.

But…guess what? To get there, the great Ted Williams struck out 709 times in his career.[50]

Imagine facing 709 failures at bat, yet those failures become a stepping stone to success. Here's a story of a man who, despite the odds, left the dugout, stood at the plate, and faced another flaming fastball, swinging away.

Michael Jordan, arguably the G.O.A.T.—Greatest of All Time—of basketball, said of his fantastic career, "I've missed over 9,000 shots in my career. I've lost almost 300 games. Twenty-six times, I've been trusted to take the game-winning shot and missed. I've failed over and over and over again in my life. And **that is why I succeed**."[51]

What kept Michael Jordan going to become one of the greatest players of all time?

He took the next shot.

Missionary, no matter how many times things, situations, people, or places discourage you, get up, swing again. Take another shot.

If I go down, I'd rather go out swinging than sitting on the bench wondering what might have been. How about you?

How many shots have you missed? How many times did you swing away at the plate and strike out? Are you going to take another shot? Attempt another at-bat? What's behind your smile that keeps you from making another go of it? Another attempt at seeking forgiveness. Another project after your last one failed. Trusting people again after another disappointing betrayal.

 Moving Forward: Take the next shot! I'd rather take another shot and miss than never play that game. How about you? Many who refused to give up fill faith's coliseum. Will you take the next shot? Become part of an elite group of attempters who, no matter how many failures, never give up?

Missionary, get up to the plate again.

Swing away again and again.

Get off that bench of disappointment and doubt. Take another shot.

He heals the brokenhearted and
bandages their wounds. He counts the stars and calls
them all by name. How great is our Lord!
His power is absolute!

Psalm 147:3-5

Required
Re-Routes

A FRIEND OF MINE WORKS in internet networking technology. Now, I understand very little about this discipline, but listening to his friends converse on the subject fascinates me.

From what I understand, he works with a team of network technicians and engineers who specialize in developing network systems by which information travels through local area networks, LAN, wide area networks, WAN, cloud networks, servers, and other data communications networks. Basically, they develop avenues by which we receive most of our information from providers to our computers.[52]

From what I've learned, there are three basic approaches to engineering networking: **static, dynamic**, and **hybrid.**

My sister, an expert in this field, explained it to me using the example of driving a car through traffic. She texted:

> I would liken it back to the day before cell phones and GPS. Back in the day, when getting stuck in a traffic jam and you didn't know any other routes, you stayed stuck in that traffic for fear of taking another route resulting in even a longer delay. Same route every time, no rerouting, static or forced—no or go.

> But now you can create dynamic routes and other ways that are free from traffic, and the plan makes you confident about taking the risk.[53]

Dynamic routing can help avoid "collisions," which occur when packets of data in transit, actively moving from one location to the another, drop the packets, causing a loss of data.[54,55]

A friend, specialist in this field, explained:

Static: Static routing involves manually configuring the routing table with fixed paths to various networks. These routes do not change unless manually updated by a network administrator.

Dynamic: Dynamic or Adaptive routing uses routing protocols to automatically update and maintain the routing table based on network topology and conditions. Routers share information to find the best path to each destination.

Hybrid: Hybrid routing combines static and dynamic routing elements to optimize network performance and management. It allows for manual route configurations while also utilizing dynamic protocols for adaptability.[56]

Upon hearing conversations on the subject, I thought, "That's a lot like missionaries! A verse came to mind.

We can make our plans, but the LORD determines our steps.

Proverbs 16:9

In other words, required reroutes will occur. Missionary life is all about routes and rerouting, ways of thinking, ministry, methodology, and life change.

The demands upon us for rerouting are continual.

Let's think about this in missionary terms. Ok? Missionaries are a unique breed. And we'll pattern ourselves, perhaps unknowingly, in static, dynamic, or hybrid routes of lifestyles, practices, and choices. But first...

The Default Gospel. The Gospel, Good News, is embedded in the person of Jesus Christ. Christ's life and obedience to his Father, willingly submitting himself to death on that old rugged cross, atones or covers over our sins, redeems us—making us faultless before God.

The default of the Gospel: Jesus told him, "I am the way, the truth, and the life. *No one can come to the Father except through me.*" John 14:6

Jesus is the Gospel, our preset configuration. This never changes. It's the default setting of our lives and work. How we live, work, and serve may vary, but the Gospel message of Jesus Christ must not.

Static Missions. When beginning our missionary lives, default settings are always preset from which we view and act upon missionary life and work. It's frequently a necessity because our training, preparation, and ethnocentricities demand it to be so.

There's no harm, no foul, here. It's what we know, who we are, how we think, and how we intend to work, and that's okay.

However, static often implies only one route to reach a desired destination, point, or task, forcing all others upon a monocultural road—the missionaries' road.

We do this because we've done it this way before, and we'll continue doing it this way, regardless. It's our default way of thinking. How often do we find ourselves here?

In technology, default refers to a system, software, or device's preset or standard configuration, setting, or behavior. It's what you get out of the box before making any customizations or changes.[57]

Your computer's default settings are essential in the beginning. But do we leave those computers in factory default settings indefinitely? Never.

It's like Windows XP. I hung onto that beautiful, stable system until the very end. Once Microsoft stopped sending updates, security patches, and vendor support, I had to decide whether to continue in Windows XP's default mode, which prevented me from upgrading software, security, and other features, or move to Windows 10.

So, I upgraded to Windows 10. It was not without pain, let me tell you, but necessary. Holding onto Windows 10 and resisting Microsoft's strong, relenting assault on upgrading to Windows 11 finds me in the same position again.

Now, they're talking about Windows 12 with Artificial Intelligence (AI). And soon, I'm sure, Windows 13, 14, and 15 into infinity and beyond!

I wouldn't say I like these changes because they make me rethink, reorder, and redeploy my rationality and actions. Most of all, they steal time from my life by making changes I'd rather not make.

Missionary ministry resembles that same dilemma. Stay the course of what you already know, no matter what, or upgrade.

Yet, many missionaries continue to operate with a Windows XP mentality. And some of us go way back to Windows Vista! Huh...

It reminds me of the Commodore Computer. The Commodore, what? Google it.

Commodore was the largest personal computer manufacturer in the past—way back like in the 80s, which in computer technology was eras and light years ago. It has been listed in the Guinness World Records as the highest-selling single-computer model ever.[58]

Now, get ready for this! The Commodore 64 personal computer sported a processing capacity of an 8-bit processor with 64 kilobytes of RAM. Intrigued yet?[59]

Here's the selling point: It had no hard drive and could not store personal data. But not to fear! You could always store up to 170 kilobytes of personal data on a 3&1/2-inch floppy drive connected to an expansion port.

How could you use that cutting-edge technology of that day today? What could you do with it?

Absolutely nothing.

Zero, zilch, nada.

Do you know any missionaries designing updates and reports on Commodore 64 computers? No?

Why?

Self-obvious.

Right?

Okay, let's wade into the doo-doo here.

Many of us paddle into our missionary works based upon default thinking, operating in static modes of previous missionary eras, depending on whether you're a Boomer, Generation X, Millennial, or Gen Z, with Gen Alpha making up the rear guard.

By the way, Gen Alpha is the first generation to be born entirely in the 21st Century and will become the largest population group ever, with over two billion people.

But…some of the most frustrated missionaries I've met often cling to outdated methods and models of missionary life and work of previous generations. For some missionaries, it's all they know. Other times, fear of change keeps them shackled to outdated, ineffective modes.

I remember a legendary missiology professor whose class I took during my first year of missionary training. The grand old gentleman, in his early sixties, prepared us for our upcoming first terms in our respective fields. I highly respected him and considered him my friend.

In my first year, he handed out a list to every mission student and shared what we needed to pack in our crates. "You must ship a crate to the field," he insisted. One big problem, however.

He and his wife began their first term of service in the Congo in the 1950s. I attended his class in 1976 but did not reach South Africa until 1986.

Many of those students shipped crates they didn't need with stuff they couldn't use, raising and wasting thousands of dollars they desperately needed.

My friend, what worked in the 80s and 90s in missions may resemble that old Commodore Computer.

The Commodore 64 stuff in the age of the Vintage Tandy 3800 HD / 25-3533—Monochrome Laptop which was my laptop of choice in the early 1990s.

Hey, by the way, I can offer you a great deal on a used laptop. Interested?

Brutal honesty, what can I offer from my era, as an aging Boomer, to Xers, Millennials, and Generation Zs that can benefit them?

I can offer them myself—a compassionate listener who can help them forge ahead on their own path to share Jesus with the nations.

But missions has changed monumentally in the past forty years. And that's okay because change is necessary. Nothing except Jesus, the Way of all Ways, never changes.

When we first embarked on our ministry among the Zulu people, our approach to missions was ethnocentric. This meant we were evaluating and understanding other cultures solely through the lens of our own culture, a perspective that was deeply ingrained in us at the time.[60] This required a shift.

Dynamic or Adaptive Missions. Soon, it became clear that Zulu culture and their way of doing things differed considerably from my preconceived notions of how things should be done. We began making the necessary adjustments.

With the Gospel at the Center, we ceded leadership to our Zulu congregations. It was glorious to see them equipped with the necessary tools to teach God's Word, sharing the hope found in Jesus Christ.

Our churches became their churches, led by Zulu people, reflecting their culture while remaining true to declaring Jesus the Way, the Truth, and the Life. The church no longer felt American.

It marked a win-win.

Before, the missionary pretty much led and managed the entirety of the ministry. This was a static approach, the only way I knew how to do missions. A dynamic, adaptive, multidirectional approach began to advance the Gospel's command more efficiently.

Zulu leaders initiated outreach programs I'd never dreamed of. Before you knew it, I sat alongside leadership instead of constantly in front. Our churches no longer depended upon me, becoming self-sufficient and self-activating.

Hybrid Missions. Our static mission approach based itself upon one methodology: me sharing Jesus among Zulu communities. Changing to dynamic shifted ownership to African leadership within the churches.

'Church' was going well. We bathed in our contentment, watching Zulu people reach their people for Christ.

Yet, we continually noticed the plight of children orphaned by the AIDS pandemic, which went unaddressed by our churches. So, I had a plan.

I've always got a plan.

We branched into Hybrid Missions when we partnered with MANNA Worldwide. We no longer struggled to find funds and resources to feed the teams of orphan children overwhelming our churches. Now, MANNA provided funds for those meals while we partnered with another source to raise funds to construct a feeding center.

Orphan children would show up before and after school for a meal. For many, it was the only nourishment they'd receive for the day.

This fed a steady stream of mothers into our churches to see the 'church' that cared for children. Oh, and many of the kids attended, too.

Our feeding and training center, a sprawling 25,000-square-foot facility, evolved into an educational training hub. It houses a daycare, kitchen, feeding center, nursery, library, and offices, with ample space for further expansion.

Changing South African laws led us to register the Training Center with the government under the Mkhamba Gardens Development Trust. This required a board of directors as we selected South African professionals to oversee the Training Center.

Then, according to South African law, I had to step down. The new law stated that only South Africans could head up such entities.

And there, we walked away from a ministry we'd poured twenty-two years into.

How's it doing today? Splendidly. It is all led and funded by South Africans.

That marked our Hybrid ministry win.

Required Reroutes

Don't know how to make it work? Learn. Don't be the missionary who envies the success of others. Instead, sit down with those achievements and ask, "Hey there, my friend, what exactly are you doing to make your ministry work?"

"How are you reaching people?"

"May I come and spend time with you, observing the form and function used to do what you so successfully do?"

Find newer sources of information in cross-cultural communications.

Study successful missionaries of the present.

Take a class.

Attend a conference.

Look at other faith groups, too. You don't need to agree with their theology to gain helpful insights.

> *Don't be the missionary who envies other's success.*

What about different ways of utilizing teams?
How do you avoid burnout?
The changing faces of healthcare in missions.
Generation-to-generation mentoring models.
How do successful businesses and business-people operate in your theatre of service?

Adapt, adapt, adapt.

 Look beyond the surface of that smile, where disappointment, uncertainty, or envy may be hiding. Reflect, "How am I doing now? What adjustments can I make? What is truly valuable? What needs to change? What is non-negotiable? Keep moving forward.

I visited a missionary in the Philippines. He was a polarizing personality, having received both praise and criticism. Some insinuated that he inflated the number of people attending his churches and camps.

During my visit to the camp, I witnessed over 1,000 Filipino teens gather at camp for a week. This occurred every week. So, when he reported that over 500,000 teens attended camps every year, if anything, he underestimated the count.

Some methods utilized at that camp, such as pyrotechnics, were cutting-edge approaches to bringing teens to Jesus. I was intrigued by their care and thoroughness in coaching teens to Jesus, but they'd outgrown their facilities.

It was time to build. How? When? Where? And who will build it?

Imagine you're building camp facilities there, such as a cafeteria or a mess hall. Before you sit, all the materials you need to build. Everything from cement to roofing materials, stoves to refrigerators, tables to chairs—it's all there. It's time to construct a building.

Now, time to strategize. You've decided to follow a preconfigured static route using volunteers from your passport country. The goal is to reach the destination of a beautifully finished new eating facility. This is the 'tried and tested' method you've always seen done before. So, with this plan, you proceed:

Building plans → Materials → <u>Volunteers</u> = New facility

Your volunteers represent your static route of completing the camp's dining hall.

After all, it makes sense.

You know these people, their competencies, and their capabilities, so you'll have better control over the project. Besides, most of these helpers come from churches that support the project financially.

One static route for a camp dining hall guides the venture toward its completion.

But a series of monumental problems arise. You soon discover that your volunteers need more skills beyond manual labor. A capable builder accompanied them, but the volunteers stood in bewilderment as he gave instructions. Their skill sets went little further than shoveling dirt or painting a room.

And the builder from overseas didn't understand the standards and compliances of the Philippines.

Frustration...

But this is your static route of choice. You are committed and stuck with it. You've got options but very few.

The project was eventually completed two years behind schedule and way over budget.

They reached an unsatisfactory conclusion, forcing the project through a limited route, which unfortunately failed. The new dining hall was almost functionless. Watching this unfold taught me the importance of diversifying our approaches and preparing for unforeseen challenges.

Sometimes, the static model is best. I know of many projects that missionaries complete using a static approach. However, I've also witnessed disasters, too.

Dynamic Missions. Dynamic routing uses real-time data and considers many factors that could impact the route, while static routing uses a prefix of set data.[61]

Dynamic is much easier and more flexible. It allows it to tolerate and develop its own routes. However, Static is a forceful go-or-no-go, and configuring it to verify connections and settings costs more and takes much longer to set up.[62]

Dynamic is set up in advance. With Static, you must network with all groups involved to make sure everything communicates.[63,64]

Dynamic Ministry makes multiple adjustments in real-time, reaching not only one solitary goal but also accomplishing a multiplicity of objectives, thereby enhancing other possibilities.

Maybe I'm pushing the analogy too far, but we have an application here.

Let's return to that same camp setting. Now, another missionary attempts a similar project, entertaining several design possibilities from various architects. This requires complex thinking, decision-making, and time.

Before beginning the project, the missionary weighs efficiency, costs, aesthetics, style, building codes, regulations, required labor, cost of materials, maintenance, energy consumption, and functionality.

Then, efficiency and impact are carefully considered. How might the facility improve accommodation and the flow of campers, and what about its longevity?

What is the projected cost? Possible over expenditures and unanticipated overruns? Does the current support base have the capacity for anticipated additional funds? Will the project depend upon a single revenue source, or can individuals and businesses be approached rather than just church councils?

Could a fund-raising Facebook page garner extra funds, create a new awareness of the camp outreach, or maybe a spare-change drive among churches back home might bring in additional donations.

So, boom! The foundations were poured, and the dining hall was completed. Perfect!

The ministry exploded with growth, surpassing all current accommodations at the camp. Building further facilities at the camp became unviable, as no more land was available.

Offices were needed for an ever-growing staff far exceeding the camp ministry. Constructing an office facility in the capitol was financially out of reach.

This necessitated a **hybrid** approach. A paradigm shift—some real out-of-the-box thinking.

The Missionary contacted a Foundation. A new partnership secured the entire eighth floor of a Medical Plaza Building in Manila, Philippines.

There, the headquarters, Global Surge, exists as a church-planting urban ministry committed to reaching this generation for Christ and transforming them into reproducing disciples who will reach the world.

Global Surge sends Filipino missionaries worldwide and trains thousands through its institutes, colleges, and universities.

Many of us don't possess the ability to do hybrid routing in our ministries, and that's okay. Stay with what you know. After all, we

112

are who we are according to the gifts and capabilities God bestows upon each one of us. You can't do what you don't know or possess.

Challenge: strive for a dynamic mode of service and ministry. Learn from others. Adjust your approach. Change tactics. Watch those more successful than you. Enable leaders.

An excellent example of Dynamic Ministry exists in the Apostle Paul.

1st, Paul held to a robust and concise commitment to Christ.

I have had *one message for* Jews and Greeks alike—the necessity of repenting from sin and turning to God, and of having faith in our Lord Jesus.

Acts 20:21

2nd, Paul possess a deep awareness of his vocation. For Paul, missions originate from the call of God.[65]

Then he told me, 'The God of our ancestors has chosen you to know his will and to see the Righteous One and hear him speak. For you are to be his witness, telling everyone what you have seen and heard.

Acts 22:14-15

3rd, Paul showed fantastic adaptability. As far as I know, his sermon, *To the Unknown God*, has never been repeated.[66]

So Paul, standing before the council, addressed them as follows: 'Men of Athens, I notice that you are very religious in every way, for as I was walking along I saw your many shrines. And one of your altars had this inscription on it: To an Unknown God. This God, whom you worship without knowing, is the one I'm telling you about.'

Acts 17:22-23

113

4th **Paul cultivated a flexible approach to missions.** Missions demand creative, insightful approaches to evangelism.[67]

Ephesus in Acts 19 involved a multifaceted tactic. He preached in synagogues, homes, and public places, attempting to build a path towards the Good News of Christ.

Acts 17:22-31 recounts Paul's celebrated speech in the Areopagus, the central meeting place in Athens, the cultural capital of the Greek islands.

He refers to the philosopher-poet Epimenides.

Paul moved from familiar places to unfamiliar places.

Paul's sensitivities and adaptation to sharing the Gospel become evident and essential in new situations. Communicating cross-culturally, he articulated the hope in Jesus Christ.

Paul is a clear example of moving from a static posture of being a 'Pharisee of Pharisees' towards a dynamic conversion to Christ on the Road to Damascus.

He became a Jewish Christ-follower, combining his ethnic individuality and religious self into a hybrid Christian identity. We see this in Philippians 1:15–18.[68]

Paul's new identity in Christ propelled him into a remarkably adaptable missionary life and ministry. He was 'flexible' in his approach, becoming all things to all people in his mission to lead them to faith in Christ.

We are called to do the same.

When I am with those who are weak, I share their weakness,
for I want to bring the weak to Christ.
Yes, I try to find common ground with everyone,
doing everything I can to save some.

1 Corinthians 9:22

Social Media
Deviations

A MISSIONARY FRIEND SERVING IN EUROPE Facebooked this message yesterday:

> Living overseas, December has always been a source of extreme loneliness and depressive episodes for me, which impact me far into January and sometimes February. So I wanted to be proactive in CHANGING THAT... Starting tomorrow, I'm saying ADIOS to all social media until at least January 7th since that's when the holidays end here.

Social media is a blessed cursedness. On one hand, we can keep up with family and friends; on the other, we're constantly reminded we're apart from F & Fs—family and friends.

Only email existed when our sons returned to the States in Florida to begin university. Because of severe criticism from university students, leadership blocked all email accessibility.

Besides a few phone calls, we had minuscule contact with our sons during their university years, apart from flying the 17,000-mile round-trip journey from Johannesburg to Pensacola to see them.

We wished Facetime, WhatsApp, Zoom, and other such media so common today existed. We missed out, felt cheated from family memories. Our hearts ached.

However, watching over two decades of social media exposure among missionaries convinces me that it presents both consequential advantages and disadvantages.

 I try to put on a happy face, but during the holidays, I've been bitten a time or two watching our sons celebrate without us. Because of the distance and my waning health, fifty-hour round-trip drives to see everyone present underlying obstacles.

With sixteen grandchildren, our sons and their families can barely afford such trips. It reminds me of an old saying: "A son is a son until he takes a wife—but a daughter is a daughter all of her life."[69]

This is the fault of no one. It was so from the beginning, "This explains why a man leaves his father and mother and is joined to his wife, and the two are united into one." Genesis 2:24

When I look at photos of my sons and their families and friends as Thanksgiving and Christmas approaches, I usually suppress my pouty, sulky spirit.

Look at all I'm missing out on?!

The missionary life is so stinking sacrificial!

But really, what am I missing out on? Yes, I'd like to be there during the physical get-togethers, but...all three sons call us on Christmas for lengthy holiday chats. Usually, I'll talk with a half dozen of our grandchildren, too. Those conversations always end, "Papa, I love you. I miss you."

It begs the question, "What are you actually missing out on?"

A simple emotional equation:

Fear + Of + Missing + Out = Farsickness^2 (Family & Friend's)

FOMO, fear of missing out, develops from a subliminal ache of approaching physical separation from Family & Friends into a chronic anxiety about all we're missing out on apart from others.

117

Giving an appearance that all is well, FOMO can become a missionary's Achilles' heel. For some, it presents the most challenging part of missionary life, driving bouts of depression and unhappiness. But we must not let on. Hey?

Consider reflecting upon a few questions that may apply ointment on familial sores when surviving Farsickness.

Consideration #1 - What am I missing out on… really?

Ok, yes, you're not physically present. Got yah, been there, and here again; it's November-December as I write this chapter, so here's how I deal with the holiday missionary blues.

In my absence, I'm never-the-less present. Does a connection with family still exist? Will you not speak with friends, message each other or video chat?

Those chats will likely occur multiple times with many individuals rather than in one large gathering. A place where everyone competes for verbal recognition. Hum…?

That's the way it was in my family growing up. Mingo's, we're known as yackers. Competition for the Attention Dominator Trophy drove noise to piercing levels. So, too, there was always that one family member who plundered everyone's emotions. Every family has one of those.

> *What are you missing out on really?*

After arriving on the field, those family holiday blow-ups never arose because we were absent! You know, where someone gets mad and storms away, lashing out with verbal insults.

You don't have any of those? Good for you. Your family is a rarity.

Our absences during the holidays resulted in various communiques: letters, cards, calls, emails, and extended video chats as technology developed, driving a sincere appreciation for each other.

This proved far more enjoyable than traveling through countries and airports, renting cars, driving for hours, and sleeping in uncomfortable places trying to see everyone.

As celebrated celebrities, in those days, we came home once every four years, we became the center of attention. Everyone wanted a piece of us. Got to tell you, I relished it.

We got better presents, too. And my bag of African trinkets for Christmas gifts surpassed everyone else's. With our three boys, Kathy and I usually ended up at the top of that ladder there.

But more so, our separation deepened our relationships as we grew to appreciate each other because of long periods of separation.

Now, when our sons started going off to college in the States, well, that was a different story. Saving years in advance allowed us to fly our sons home to South Africa for Christmas or us to them. Wow…great times.

Ponder: How can FOMO help you discover the goodness happening around you? Appreciate your family and friends. Are you growing deeper in relationships because of social media's benefits?

Most of all, how can FOMO help draw you closer to God?

If Jesus stood with us today, he might say, "So let not FOMO trouble your hearts… you believe in God… how about believing in me also."

And what if Jesus finished this caution as he did in his Sermon on the Mount, "FOMO dominate the thoughts of unbelievers, but your heavenly Father already knows all your needs." Matthew 6:32

Consideration #2 – How can social media help lessen FOMO?

I once spoke with Lyle Mahon, a missionary in South Africa. He is the grandson of Edgar Mahon, the founder of Mahon Mission.

We both commented on the amenities younger missionaries enjoyed that didn't exist during the three generations of Mahon missionaries.

While standing with me in the foothills of Kwazulu, Natal, Lyle remarked, "It doesn't seem to help keep missionaries on the field. The first mention of home, we'll never see them again."

Too true.

However, social media can also fortify us against FOMO. Consider that such capabilities never existed to communicate with family and friends as they do today. How lucky we are.

Last month, we enjoyed video conversations with missionaries in Europe, Asia, and Africa.

The privilege we enjoy! We can talk with anyone, almost anywhere. While serving thousands of miles away from each other, staying in touch has never been easier.

Social media can become a friend if you focus on its benefits. Or the worst companion when entering into its dark world.

Question #3 - What benefits and experiences does the missionary lifestyle provide that families and friends back home miss out on?

For me, missionary life provides the freedom of not being confined to an office or cubicle, stuck in a droning, repetitious job working for the man. It's a lifestyle that many envy. How about you?

One missionary couple shared. "When back home, my sister always talks about taking her kids to the mall." Like, that's such a big deal. After a while, her droning wears on me.

I replied, "We took our girls to Madrid, Spain, to see the Real Madrid Soccer Club play for the UEFA championship. Afterward, we went to Madrid Xanadú Shopping Centre, where we watched the kids snow ski inside the mall as we drank coffee."

She winked. That shut her up."

What About You?

Benefits of Missionary Life	Your FOMO +/-

How do your missionary experiences outweigh FOMO? There's no other life like it!

_____

_____

_____

_____

_____

 What about embracing all the benefits social media provides over your FOMO? See it as a plus rather than allow its distractions to pull your emotions off course.

The LORD is my light and my salvation—
so why should I be afraid?

Psalm 27:1a

Spiritual
Shrivelings

ALMOST EVERY MISSIONARY I'VE KNOWN, including myself, experiences seasons of spiritual shriveling, an emptiness. Slogging away in the breaking waves of missionary work, we often face seasons when our soul's sails hang limp.

Ever been there? You're there now? Take heart. We've all been there at one time or another.

Good news! God is aware! The Bible offers much help concerning this, too. And many examples exist in the Bible of those who encountered such challenges during their voyages.

Job: lost everything: a good wife, family, name, health, and wealth.

Hagar: an enslaved, abandoned single parent left to die.

Joseph: sold into slavery by family members.

Moses: sent on a disciplinary desert journey.

Ruth: lost financial means to support herself.

Elijah: talking to himself in a cave.

Hanna: struggled for years with infertility.

David: abandoned by friends.

Hosea: a cheating spouse.

Jeremiah: Lost everything because of an evil king.

Ester: married a foreigner and faced an ultimate dilemma.

Mary: I'm pregnant, but really, I've never…

Peter: Jesus, who's Jesus? I don't know him. I DO NOT KNOW HIM!

Sometimes our soul enters the land of 'Meh...' You know, when life becomes lackluster, battered by the *blahs*.

While the Land of Spiritual Meh may seem desolate and directionless, it is also a potential ground for transformation. It's a place where we can learn to weather temptation's squalls and emerge sturdier.

It's in these challenging times that, perhaps, our most significant opportunities for growth exist.

What are the critical ingredients for getting through such times? For revitalizing our souls. So that:

God seems real again.

The Bible comes alive.

We see people in God's image.

Coming together with fellow followers of Jesus is not just a duty, but a wellspring of joy and strength. It's a place where we find solace, understanding, and share in spiritual experiences.

Prayer turns from mumbling into an honest conversation with the Creator, during which we can love and want to serve again.

The Land of Meh – Faith's Best Opportunity

Four laid-out principles exist to explain faith—four steps that will invigorate your faith. These four steps are found in one verse of the Bible.

Faith shows us the "reality of what we hope for; evidence for what we cannot see." Hebrews 11:1

When you find yourself in the Land of Meh, look to God. Remember, faith is not just a belief; it's a powerful force that brings God pleasure. You have to want it—you have to want it bad!

124

You see, the Land of Meh says, "Ah, maybe it's all a facade. God's not real. You really can't see any fruit from your labors. Where's God anyway? What you're doing is not worth your time. It won't amount to anything. Give it up." Blah... Faith, however, proves the opposite.

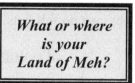

What or where is your Land of Meh?

Faith's Realm

Faith kicks the Land of Meh in the teeth, sending a bulldozer to demolish it. Faith is a giant slayer of doubt and spiritual lethargy.

Faith satisfies spiritual barrenness. Faith fills empty pots to the brim.

During seasons of spiritual dryness, faith fills our sails with the winds of confidence.

Confidence in no matter how you feel, God is real, involved, and pleased.

However, that type of faith must be pure and complete. Genuine God-pleasing faith requires 4 steps.

And it is <u>impossible</u> to [1]please God <u>without</u> faith. Anyone who [2]wants to come to him [3]must believe that God exists and that [4]he rewards those who sincerely seek him.

Hebrews 11:6

4 Steps of Full Faith

#1—Faith wants God's pleasure. Faith is the key to pleasing God, and pleasing God becomes the priority. Anything we attempt, think, or do for God only brings pleasure when embedded in faith.

125

Missionary, here's a sobering thought. Could some of our missionary activities, not pleasure God because our motives for doing what we do fall outside of faith?

...it is <u>impossible</u> <u>to</u> [1] <u>please</u> <u>God</u> **without faith.**

The first mark of authentic faith is a deep, unrelenting desire for God. This faith makes our labors of love well pleasing to the Great I Am. Do you wish to become well-pleasing to God?[70]

There was a Wendy's® commercial in the 1970s where two ancient women stood at a hamburger competitor's counter, looking down on a pathetic piece of meat after removing the top bun from their hamburger. They pressed a nagging repetitive phrase, "WHERE'S THE BEEF?"

I don't know how often I embarked on successful projects without a wink of faith—my energy and abilities alone to influence people and raise funds marked many successful ventures. Looking back, I ask myself:

Where's the Faith?
Where's the Faith?
Where's the Faith?

#2—Faith wants God's presence. Missionary, Pastor, Christian worker, what do you desire more than anything else? Remember Jesus' words, "Wherever your treasure is, there the desires of your heart will also be." Matthew 6:21

 Where do your treasures lie? Money doesn't look for God. Popularity seeks its own recognition. Power wishes to exploit others. And, well, sometimes, we missionaries find ourselves on stages before people, competing with other missionaries, trying to gain acceptance, support, and recognition worthy of consideration above others. It's the smile that can win them over to our cause.

Anyone who [2] **wants** to come to him...

What are your biggest wants?

- _____

- _____

- _____

- _____

Now, where or how does God fit into all this?

#3—Faith wants God's person. We'll all nod, "I believe in God." But when was the last time you faced an immense challenge and responded like an agnostic? Yep, a Christian agnostic.

Have you ever stopped to consider how often we respond to life's challenges without acknowledging the presence of our Jehovah Jireh? When we allow emotions to say God's not interested or concerned with my life, plight, or problems.

At the heart of agnosticism lies a profound paradox; it suggests that if God exists, his nature is inherently unknowable to us.

But faith is not passive. It yearns for God. Faith craves his presence. It strives to draw near to him, steadfast in the belief that God is not distant, but intimately present, a comforting truth regardless of the circumstances we find ourselves in.

Faith insists we:

³ must **believe** that **God exists...**

#4 – **Faith wants God's presents.** Yeah, that's right, presents, gifts. Faith seeks God's rewards. Is this Prosperity Gospel?[71] No, it's a simple fact of faith claimed in the Scriptures.

⁴ he **rewards** those who sincerely seek him.

During my darkest, most difficult times battling PTSD, seven simple words appeared in my journal, *"God Rewards Don When Don Seeks Him."*

A faith shift occurred while in The Valley of My Shadow of Death.

Rather than circling around critical belief systems instilled into me, my soul's sails filled, moving towards God. As I sought pleasure in God, God reciprocated.[72]

God became my Rewarder. The New American Standard Bible translates the verse, "He is a **rewarder** of those who seek Him." The word 'rewarder' spurred an adventurer's spirit to discover more!

Here, the thrust of 'rewarder' carries the idea of paying wages. An older word usage is 'recompense.' To recompense, repay one for their activities, labors, or efforts. [73,74]

To pay a wage.[75]

In the first thirty-four verses of the eleventh chapter of Hebrews, you'll find those who prospered doing great works of faith. God recompensed them well.

But in the last half of the chapter, you'll also find people who didn't seem to fare so well. Yet, they did so by faith.

They died.

Were sawn in half.

Starved.

Displaced.

Tortured.

Whipped.

Mocked.

Killed by the sword.

Mistreated.

Destitute.

Hiding in caves and holes in the ground.

Wandering over deserts and mountains.

Yet,

Recompensed

All these people earned a good reputation *because of their faith,* yet none of them received all that God had promised.

Hebrews 11:39

What do we learn here? Faith doesn't pledge a life above persecution, poverty, sickness, or death.

Instead, it implies a deep satisfaction with God, who rewards our acts of faith. According to Hebrews 11, these rewards, recompenses, compensations, and gifts don't necessarily all come in this life but follow in the next.

I can't fully understand or explain this. I just accept and believe it by faith.

And maybe, just maybe, when we find ourselves pulling in empty nets, it's because we fail to focus on God, accept our situation, and carry on by faith regardless.

129

Moving forward: Anger, bitterness, sadness, trauma, apathy, sarcasm, and whatever can fill voids apart from faith. But instead, let faith fill your empty nets and hollow places.

Allow God to recompense you with the fruit of his presence: love, joy, peace, patience, kindness, goodness, faithfulness, gentleness, and self-control. Galatians 5:22b-23

Focus on God's presence in every aspect of life, relying upon his spirit to fill any hollow places.

What fills your empty places?

O God, you are my God; I earnestly search for you.
My soul thirsts for you; my whole body longs
for you in this parched and weary
land where there is no water.

Psalm 63:1

Tantalizing
Temptations

Satan rose up against Israel and **incited** David to take a census of Israel. So David said to Joab and the commanders of the troops, 'Go and count the Israelites from Beersheba to Dan. Then report back to me so that I may know how many there are.'

1 Chronicles 21:1 NIV

OVER A THIRTY-YEAR MISSIONARY CAREER, I've witnessed droves of shipwrecked missionary lives, families, and ministries who succumbed to their temptations.

Temptation doesn't always mean giving in to lust and vices, which is how we often view it. Temptation comes from the Greek word *peirasmos*. The NIV translates *peirasmos* into these English words:

temptation x 8,
trials x 4,
trial x 3,
testing x 2,
severe testing x 1,
tempted x 1,
tempting x 1,
test x 1. [76]

Temptation can also include challenges, circumstances, and severe testings. Let's look at this situation with David.

Satan rose up against Israel and **incited,** David to take a census of Israel.

Remember that the Old Testament Scriptures were written in Hebrew, not English. Here, 'incited' / *çûwth*, a Hebrew word, comes with many shades of meaning.[77, 78]

The Brown-Driver-Briggs Hebrew and English Lexicon		Strong's Exhaustive Concordance and English Lexicon
Hebrew word: וַיָּסֶת çûwth	*Hiphil* stem	Possibly from: שַׁיִת shayith
allure	to incite *to a request*	Prick, as in a thorn bush
instigate	to allure, lure	seduce
entice	to instigate (*bad sense*)	stimulate

Satan tested, lured, enticed, stimulated, instigated, and pricked David. To what end? It was just a census. What's the big hairy deal? What's behind a decision decides its value or detriment.

First, "Satan rose up against Israel." David, the king of Israel, would lead his people to a disastrous decision touching the entire nation. On the surface, a census in itself mattered little. However, the agent behind the census, Satan, lured David into doing something besides just counting the population.

Perhaps it was a matter of pride or arrogance on David's part—look how many warriors I've got! Even Joab, a sin-warped person, warned David of the severe consequences of his actions. David refused to listen.

Ever done that before?

What test is before you at this moment?

Are you sure you want to make the decision?

Make that move?

Buy that thing?

Carry that attitude toward another missionary, pastor, Christian, or family member?

Look at that smartphone again?

View those images?

Touch that woman?

Damage another missionary's work?

Pan off your Bible reading again?

Going another day, week, month, or year without a meaningful conversation with God?

Putting off something you need to make right?

What heart-wrenching accounts do you know of that scatter ministry's tides and currents with defrocked, discouraged, or damaged missionaries? Those who left desolate spiritual wakes in their departures.

 Seasons of spiritual dryness—when we're at our weakest—provide Satan's best opportunity to strike. Behind our smiles, we can stroke corrupt tendencies, make poor choices, stray from our spiritual disciplines, becoming insensitive to the presence of God. Then expect the enemy to strike. And strike hard.

You never attack an enemy at its strongest position. Satan, an exceptional tactician, always tries to set the place, means, time, and agenda to confront us during our weakest moments.

He approached Jesus in this manner.

At the end of Jesus' forty-day fast, Satan presents 3 temptations to Christ. How did Christ overcome? Pass the test? Get through the allurements? Matthew 4:1-11

Yes, ok, being the Son of God helped, but remember, forty days with no food.

Jesus, in a physically weakened state, presented a perceived susceptibility to tempt Jesus that the enemy couldn't resist. And what battle position did Jesus use to defeat the enemy? He quoted Old Testament Scripture to him. Jesus took a defensive position.

James, the half-brother of Jesus, described it this way:

Resist the devil, and he will flee from you.

James 4:7

Our most vital spiritual position should mirror Jesus. We must establish defensive *perimeters, fortifying ourselves* behind impenetrable walls of God's Word.

Our posture becomes a <u>defensive</u> <u>position</u> rather than offensive. An excellent, solid defensive position employs effective strategies against the enemy.

What defensive tactic did Jesus employ?

Each time Satan tempted Christ, **Christ held a defensive position from the Written Truth.** Jesus quoted the Scriptures to Beelzebub, the chief agent of evil and opposition to God.

Satan hates the Word, both written and incarnate. So, stand with Jesus behind God's Word, and Satan will flee.

Get into the Written Word.
Pour yourself into Prayer.
Embrace the Incarnate Word.

No **temptation** has overtaken you except what is common to mankind. And God is faithful; he will not let you be **tempted** beyond what you can bear. But when you are **tempted**, he will also provide a way out so that you can endure it.

I Corinthians 10:13 NIV

Trust in the Lord and do good; dwell in the land and enjoy safe pasture. Take delight in the Lord, and he will give you the desires of your heart.

Psalm 37:3-4 NIV

Astringent Stress

WE ATTENDED SEVERAL PRESENTATIONS, during which they shared their heartfelt calling to go to the field. Pleasant, convincing, articulate, and sincere, their sense of urgency to raise the funds necessary to move, set up, and begin life in a country thousands of miles away proved compelling. We'd become good friends with this couple.

This young, warm couple asked to meet with us just before leaving for the field. Now, I'm not saying it's normal, but take heart: many missionaries experience panic attacks.

Darla began, "I don't know what's happening. The closer we get to leaving, the more I want to crawl out of my skin."

James chimed in, "Yeah, me too, but mine is like...ah...like... pain in my chest, sometimes breathing really hard, and anxiety sort of covers over me. I don't know what's going on here."

I replied, "Darla, James, know this. This is abnormally normal. Many missionaries experience anxiety reactions to the huge amounts of stress they are under."

Together, we made a list of all the major changes they'd experienced over the last three years.

- Finishing their two-year missionary internship.
- Completing the mountain of paperwork for mission agency approval.
- Those in-depth physical and emotional evaluations.
- "You're going to do what!?" from both parents.
- Cautious warnings from friends.
- 80,000 miles of driving.
- 203 field presentations.
- Reaching their fundraising goals.
- Birth of a child.
- Selling their house and furnishings.
- Filling a crate with the few items they kept to ship overseas.
- Planning with veteran missionaries to receive them once they arrived.
- Travel plans, visas, immunizations, plane tickets, and...

After completing the list, Kathy, my wife, asked, "What do you see here."

Darla nailed it, "Stress!"

I added, "Missionary stress."

What is Stress?

While it wears many faces, *stress is a sense of being overwhelmed by a situation where you struggle to cope with its pressures.*

We all experience stress. It's a part of our daily existence. Short-lived periods of stress are normal, but *when chronic stress occurs for long periods, it becomes detrimental to health.*[79]

Missionary life fills itself with new relationships and unimaginable adventures. However, it also brings unprecedented levels of tension and strains far beyond what many others experience—stress that few missionary candidates foresee or prepare for before leaving for their fields of service.

Upon hitting the tarmac at the airport, Sent Ones enter a land that doesn't expect and rarely wants them. Dysfunctional missionary teams often make new missionaries' first arrival to the field taxing.

> *Missionary life brings unprecedented levels of stress.*

Many missionaries find themselves at an extreme disadvantage with little cognitive awareness of how to recognize or manage their new off-the-chart stress levels.

I remember our first year in South Africa. Figuring out how to do anything became stressful. We had to figure out where to rent a house, how to connect utilities, and where to set up new bank accounts.

Driving in South Africa was initially a hair-raising affair.

Enrolling our sons in school proved an arduous task, too. The people in charge of transcripts didn't understand our son's report cards and academic records. Just entering our son into kindergarten brought on a migraine.

Then, there's language acquisition. Learning the Zulu language marked more than a few hours of daily study. Even after two years, I could barely converse. At the end of our twenty-two years of service in South Africa, I was still flipping vocabulary cards of Zulu words.

One of the most stressful activities these days is the paperwork and costs of visa requirements. Many share the extensive measures required to get a visa and remain in the country God called them to.

Navigating the political unrest and rampant violence throughout the country required us to constantly look over our shoulders. Even today, living in the United States, my situational awareness mimics the apprehensions of living in South Africa. I'm always looking over my shoulder, sensing danger everywhere.

After twenty-two years of missionary service, we returned 'home,' finding little in common with American Christians. Prayer meetings often addressed nonessentials, with a little more of this and a little less of that.

Sermons lacked the New Life in Christ—the Gospel. Church gatherings differed so much from our years in Africa that we felt like visitors; we were and still are.

Seventeen years later, we still feel the same, covered in loneliness, even though we are surrounded by pastors and very good people who love us. But this is the missionary paradigm we must understand and meet.

 We're still outsiders, but we're surrounded by gracious, kind people. Yet cross-pollinating between two lives, fields, and cultures brings enormous stress, regardless of how we might ignore it or try to hide it with a smile.

One person offered me advice over coffee: "Don, your conversations are always so serious, like life-and-death stuff. People want to talk about their kids in school, pets, and favorite coffee shops, not about AIDS, world hunger, or poverty. The world is not as serious a place for us as it is to you."

Yes, we were no longer missionaries, but we couldn't separate our twenty-two years of life and ministry in South Africa from our conversations. Those experiences are part of who we are.

The demanding journey of leaving one's passport country, entering another culture, and beginning a new life can pour crushing stress upon even the most dedicated of us.

Then, leaving that country and returning to the missionary's birth country doubles that stress, at least it did for me.

But...we smile. Don't we? Well, most of the time. Sometimes. Not so much? Anymore?

Just How Stressful is Missionary Life?

Years ago, while living in South Africa, I took the Holmes-Rahe Stress Scale. They developed the test in 1967 after examining the records of 5,000 medical patients to determine whether stressful events attributed to their illnesses. Patients took the test based on 43 life events and relative scores.[80] Each life event had a numerical score.

The desired range on the Holmes-Rahe Stress Scale is around 150 points or fewer. This indicates a relatively moderate amount of life change and a low susceptibility to stress-induced health breakdown. It's a reminder of the importance of managing stress for our overall health and well-being.

A score between 150 and 300 points indicated a 50% chance of health breakdown in the next 2 years.

A score above 300 meant an 80% chance of health breakdown, according to the Holmes-Rahe statistical prediction model.[81]

When I took my test, I scored over 700.

Most missionaries land high on the Holmes Rahe Stress Test, at around 600. First-term missionaries can average 800-900! [82]

There is justifiable criticism of the Holmes Rahe Stress Test. However, it's safe to assume that missionaries experience high—almost intolerable—stress levels, which few other than missionaries can understand.

But… remember that smile. Right?

The Search for Empathy

I remember trying to share with an adult Sunday school class in Wisconsin my extreme angst about witnessing people murdered in South Africa. I mean, seeing people burned, hacked, shot, or electrocuted to death.

And let me tell you, it's a whole lot different seeing it in person than Shogun or Jason Stratham movies.

One woman piped up, "Oh, we have that all the time here. In Milwaukee, they murder people every day."

Milwaukee? An hour away from her location, a place she'd never visited nor dared step foot in, yet she could identify with me?

Once again, over the course of a four-day mission conference, I endeavored to convey the harsh realities of the sights, sounds, and smells of violence that persist in South Africa. This prompted the pastor to request a meeting with me.

He said, "Don, that's not what I want my people to hear. Just talk about souls saved, churches started, and the need to reach our new giving goal for the coming year."

I smiled, "Okay."

But INSIDE… Well, you really don't want to know what I was thinking.

I wanted to leave the conference altogether—ghost em, disappearing—but I didn't. Tried my best to keep up my missionary smile, although, with a bit of sneer, I suspect.

You know what?

Not only did the church not raise my support, but they discontinued it altogether.

Not realizing how raw and aggressive my emotions appeared, stress compromised my disposition as hairline fractures started showing. I needed help, but how, with whom, and where?

Missionary, finding someone to share your harshest experiences with is crucial. That's why:

Firefighters talk with firefighters about the fire scene.

ER nurses talk with other ER nurses about what is happening in the emergency room.

Soldiers talk with soldiers about the battlefield.

Teachers talk with teachers about the classroom.

Pastors talk with other pastors about pastoring.

Missionaries need to talk with other missionaries about missionary stuff.

What about you?

Consider the profound impact of finding a fellow missionary with whom you can share your journey. It's not just a possibility, but a necessity.

Learning to Recognize Stress

Intermountain Healthcare gives some helpful advice on recognizing stress:

> Stress is a physical and emotional response to a situation. The situation may be positive, like a new baby or a job promotion. Or it can be negative, like a traffic jam or a fight with your teenager. Your body doesn't know the difference; it just knows that something is happening and should get ready to respond.[83]

Dealing With Stress

How can we deal with stress? We all experience it daily, but long-protracted seasons wear us down. Many ways exist to tackle this demon. For me, a holistic, multi-pronged approach works best.

Avoid Excessiveness. Too much activity creates stress. Excessively involving yourself in a singular pursuit reduces time for other important considerations. While any pursuit may be good or neutral, a good thing becomes detrimental if it causes neglect in other essential areas of life.

Consider this scenario: if you make your career your sole focus, you might find yourself neglecting your family or your physical health.

Stress.

Take, for example, an individual who's always at the fitness center. Workout becomes a priority above all other considerations, and time is reduced from other activities to make room for a workout.

Stress.

It's how an addiction works. When a substance, activity, or thing becomes a chronic harmful habit altering our brain function—thinking, perspective, or attitude—an addiction is born.

Apart from the psychological ramifications of an addiction, it also affects spiritual health.

Missionaries I meet who struggle with addictions rarely express a spiritually healthy disposition. Excessiveness spawns strain and stress that dictate their lives in unhealthy directions.

And, okay, you don't take drugs or drink. Still, we can binge on Social media, movies, travel lust, fundraising—always got to get more—our favorite coffee shop…talking to the Starbuckers out there; pick your poison.

And…I like Starbucks, too, by the way, when they get my drink order right.

I've known missionaries who spent much of their time in the movie theaters or wandering the malls.

Others spend many of their days at coffee shops.

You'd find some missionaries on the golf course anytime and almost all the time. No, I don't hate golf. I used to be pretty decent at it till I lost the ability to swing a club.

And…okay, being a member of Toast Masters, Rotary International, The Quilting Bee, or anything else is alright if it doesn't become your life's prime focus or source of activity.

Balance is the key. I've noticed that stressed-out people often lack balance, ignoring critical areas of their lives.

> *Learn to manage stress or stress will manage you.*

A pastor friend attended monthly meetings with a dozen other pastors. Occasionally, I found time to pop into those gatherings. In every meeting, he spoke of a relentless pursuit of his Ph.D. He talked incessantly about the time he spent working on that degree.

Six months later, his wife served him with divorce papers. That was not only the end of his marriage. The church soon voted to dismiss him, too, leaving him unemployed. The very thing he gave himself to, he lost.

Missionary, your work—wait a minute…who's work? Please don't mistake busying yourself over sacrificing your walk with God, richness in marriage, devotion to family, relationships, self-care, and health.

Imbalance. We sacrifice the good over the best, mediocrity over good, mediocrity over often a shoddy lifestyle that leads us to not-so-good places.

 Look at your life. How balanced are your passions and priorities versus nonessentials? Life's margins are not limitless. There's only so much you can cram into a day.

When was your last physical? I CAN NOT emphasize this enough. Many times, missionaries share what they believe is depression or some other mental ailment, only to find out the source of their anxiety and stress is more physical than mental.

The two connect, but sometimes, after treating a physical ailment, mental health improves. Stress management becomes more efficient when these are in sync.

As one suffering from a long-term disabling genetic disorder, I know that physical health affects mental health and increases stress levels.

A while back, what I thought were the effects of stress, you know, that uptight sensation in the chest, turned out to be a minor heart condition and a no-so-minor blood pressure of 160 over 120. I was uptight all the time.

A thorough physical revealed this. With medication and very light exercise, blood pressure decreased to a healthy level. And boom! That stress sensation dissipated.

Missionaries, we often neglect our health, perhaps thinking our God-callings exempt us from such things.

Pay attention to your physical health. Get that yearly checkup. Don't allow busyness to rob you of life. Make your physical health a priority and stay on top of it.

How's that smile?

What about sleep? Sleep deprivation becomes a debilitating issue when it's chronic. It's easy to spot a sleep-deprived person dragging through life. Many missionaries struggle with sleep for a variety of reasons.

Monitor your sleep. If you're struggling, deal with it. Sleep is one of the best things we can do for ourselves.

Perhaps see a doctor and get a mild sedative.

Start an exercise routine.

What about taking a break? I mean, truly disconnecting from ministry and missionary work. It's not a sign of weakness, but a necessary and beneficial step to maintain your well-being. By settling your thoughts away from the stress of missionary work, you're allowing yourself to recharge.

I know a few missionaries that plan this into their yearly schedules. They jet away to another place, unplug, and refresh.

Here's a secret. Your supporters don't need to know.

AND…don't answer that phone! Don't send those text messages or answer those emails. When was the last time you did that?

A break from the News? News media worldwide focuses on the worst of the worst. One hundred years ago, most people knew only of events in their immediate vicinity, absorbing only small bits of information.

Today, however, we overload our minds with multiple events worldwide, bombarding ourselves with continuous streams of traumatic information.

TIME recently ran an article, *Watching War Unfold on Social Media Affects Your Mental Health*. In it, J. Ducharme says,

> Research suggests that news coverage of traumatic events can affect viewers' mental health—and with footage and photos from Ukraine flooding social media and misinformation spreading rampantly, that has implications for public health. [84]

> Roxane Cohen Silver, a researcher on media coverage and trauma, says, "The amount of media someone consumes and how graphic that content influences its effects on mental health." [85]

> "The best predictor for having lower anxiety and depressive symptoms was to avoid watching too much news," said Dr. Radua, a psychiatrist affiliated with King's College London and the Karolinska Institute in Sweden.[86]

Today's media landscape is bombarded with overwhelming instances that showcase humanity's worst elements.

And with social media? Do I really need to know what's going on in the lives of a dozen people I've never met? Reels on Instagram? Every Tik Toc?

Then, barrages of fake news flood social media. During the 2020 election, constant salvos of anger spilled out in people's Facebook posts. Whether Right or Left, people raged on social media. Many reactions seemed backed by fake news, which produced a constant siege mentality.

In 2024, here we are again.

How about giving the news and social media periodic breaks? Because of travel, we must be aware of world events, but perhaps it's also essential that we also create seasons of newsless environments.

Again, make time to unravel. Missionaries usually don't listen to me on this one. And here's the thing: while intended for rest, furloughs and home assignments often turn into anything but rest. Sometimes, we're <u>wound</u> so tight that the only result is snap!

Interestingly, the word '<u>wound</u>' is from the old English word 'wund' and means 'ulcer' or 'injury.' Apparently, hundreds of years ago, being wund too tight was also a problem.[87]

 When do you unwind? How do you unravel? Listening to classical music or soft jazz helps calm my mind. Exercise can help. Writing is my go-to place of respite. For Kathy, painting with watercolors eases tension. Find your calm and go there often.

Careful of over-isolation. During the Covid pandemic, we became acutely aware that long-term isolation is detrimental to mental health.

Some missionaries withdraw into seclusion. They retract themselves from everyday life, used up, worn out, and wound tight. I did this at times both as a pastor and missionary.

Short stints are healthy, but long durations of divorcing yourself from people, hiding like a hermit, becomes detrimental to mental health. Mental health affects everything.

I'm aware of a few missionaries—remember, we've spoken with thousands over the years—that present severe agoraphobic symptoms. It's "The fearing and avoiding places or situations that might cause panic and feelings of being trapped, helpless or embarrassed."[88]

Simon and Garfunkel's hit song, *I Am a Rock*, ends with:

> I am shielded in my armor
> Hiding in my room, safe within my womb,
> I touch no one, and no one touches me
> I am a rock. I am an island.
> And a rock feels no pain
> And an island never cries

Yes, a rock feels no pain, but people do. An island may never cry, but isolation, especially for those with high stress levels, rarely proves sound. And social isolation often produces people with higher levels of depression and mental disorders.[89]

Recognize your need for help. Missionaries, we're sometimes the absolute worst at seeking help, aren't we? Our constant stressful routines put us at high risk.

Also… with our bigger-than-life callings, we'd like to think we're not susceptible to health issues. That's until stress pushes us off the rails into high blood pressure, heart disease, ill health, and mental unwellness.

Being a missionary, loving Jesus, and attending to the spiritual duties of missionary life and work don't guarantee a stress-free, unhindered life.

How do you handle stress?

Remember,

Without counsel purposes are disappointed: but in the multitude of counselors they are established.

Proverbs 15:22 KJV

148

When we manage stress well, life becomes more navigable, lending itself to enjoyment and appreciation. Deal with your stress before it derails into a dungeon of despair.

Taken a Stress Test Lately?

Holmes Raye Life Stress Inventory

https://www.stress.org/wp-content/uploads/2019/04/stress-inventory-1.pdf

Mindful Stress Test

Mental Health American–Stress Screener
https://www.bemindfulonline.com/test-your-stress

Mill Creek Christian Counseling
https://www.mhanational.org/get-involved/stress-screener

5 Ways to Reduce Stress

Heather Estep, MS, LMHCA
https://millcreekchristiancounseling.com/5-ways-to-reduce-stress/

The LORD is my shepherd; I have all that I need. He lets me rest in green meadows; he leads me beside peaceful streams. He renews my strength.

Psalm 23:1-3a

Pestering
Pasts

NO MATTER WHERE YOU GO or how far the journey, past experiences accompany you.

Everyone has a past. It happened. It's in the recesses of our beautiful brains that God gives us. We can run, but we cannot hide. Our pasts are always a part of who we are.

Kathy and I both come from families that went far beyond dysfunctional. Perhaps our calling to South Africa was an unknown inner effort to get as far away from our childhoods as possible.

You know what? Being 10,000 miles away did not erase the anger I carried from my familial experiences.

Sometimes unwittingly, we head off to a new place, traveling the farthest distance from point A to point B, our newly believed reality. For a time, our A becomes a remote, forgotten existence. Yet, it resurfaces when B becomes part of A, melding the two realities into one.

> *Our pasts are always a part of us.*

If your life was a pleasant once-upon-a-time, good for you. Count your blessings. Try to recall those events during troubling episodes.

But for many of us, with pasts littered with traumatic events, forgetting becomes a colossal fruitless effort. That's because we can never entirely forget our yesterdays. Yesterday makes up our today.

Our pasts affect us both positively and negatively. Growing up with alcoholic parents, for example, fostered adverse childhood experiences—ACEs.[90] Children of alcoholics are much more likely to become addicted to alcohol or drugs.

In my *Adverse Childhood Experiences*, I scored 7 out of 10. Ten being the most severe. Kathy, my wife, had an ACE score of 9 out of 10.

Some experiences you can't shake off. Here's a thought: perhaps we can squeeze out a positive from such considerable hurdles to overcome traumatic childhood experiences.

Then there are:

Sexual abuse.

A hijacking.

An assault.

A betrayal.

A missionary team that turned against you.

Your Timothys in the ministry that disappoint you.

A missionary friend who was shot dead before your very eyes.

Spiritual abuse.

Burglaries.

The scars of severe physical abuse while growing up.

A legacy of seemingly not being liked by anyone anywhere.

The host missionary you initially worked with.

That first-time young missionary couple you hosted.

Being scared of the dark.

Experiencing physical, emotional, or spiritual neglect.

Fear a past health problem will return.

Anxiety and apprehension of how your current health issue will affect you as it progresses.

Learning to Deal With Our Pasts

Comatose realities buried deep within our minds can resurface. That episode or thing you want to forget occupies brain space.

> **Deal with your past, or your past will deal with you.**

That's because they are one.

Our past is our present.

We can't escape it.

We can try to ignore it.

Run from it.

But it's always there.

Disturbing events of childhood, inappropriate relationships, unwholesome habits, or mental deficits assail us.

It's a constant.

It's part of our being.

They become a part of who we are. Accepting this is a good step towards growth and healing.

Your past is part of your present.

However, any pain you may have suffered can become an agent to benefit yourself and others. Pain can also connect us with God rather than distancing us.

Your past may become the very thing God uses to develop you into a more effective presence.

Concerning his past, the Apostle Paul wrote:

For when I am weak, then I am strong.

2 Corinthians 12:10b

Embrace Your Past

Rather than playing hide-and-seek with the past, for me, it's best to confront it. Look it straight in the eyes. Deal with it. Acknowledge what took place. Get help navigating your brain's ability to cope with a troubled past rather than hiding behind a facade's smile. I don't want to waste my pain; I'll mold it to benefit myself and others. The past must not hold me hostage to negative emotions of self-worth.

Let God Into Your Past

153

For most of my life, I failed to see God in any of the unpleasantries of childhood.

My efforts focused on high busyness, and cramming my brain with activity. Research has proven that the brain can't think of two things simultaneously.[91] So, as long as my emotions focused on something other than the past, I was free, so I thought.

Looking back, it's clear God was present and cared for me. Not that God approved of the cruelty of it all, but I think God tracked with it, later giving purpose to my pain.

See God working in your past. See God working in you now. This is a difficult point to sell to many, even missionaries. A universal question usually occurs;

Why?

Why, God, did you let this happen to me?
Why weren't you there?
Why didn't you do this or that?
Why don't you care?

God Doesn't Care?

Many times, my anger flared toward the Almighty. I concluded that my unimportant life didn't catch God's eye enough to care about the immediacy of my troubles. However, I've come to realize the opposite is true.

Jesus identifies with our suffering. Rather than removing anguish, Christ embraced it on the cross.

This High Priest of ours **understands** our weaknesses, for *he faced all of the same testings we do,* yet he did not sin.

Hebrews 4:15 Emphasis Mine

This implies Jesus suffered with us, with you, and with me individually during our pain and dreadful situations. And…as part of the omnipotent trinity, Jesus suffers with us as we suffer, when we suffer, and where we suffer.

It reminds me of the old hymn by Johnson Oatman, *No, Not One.*

There's not a friend like the lowly Jesus,
No, not one! no, not one!
None else could heal all our soul's diseases,
No, not one! no, not one!

Jesus knows all about our struggles,
He will guide till the day is done;
There's not a friend like the lowly Jesus,
No, not one! no, not one!

Christ's life and death show the ultimate effort to redeem us, to make us worthwhile again, and to provide us with meaningful purpose in our pain.

Everything we want to be rid of and start anew lies within Jesus. Reaching out, Christ frees me from hiding in my past. My past is still present, but it doesn't possess as much control over me now.

> *Christ frees us from hiding in our pasts.*

As Jesus becomes our restorative, abundant life, His transformative power revitalizes the effects of an injurious past and grants new life.

But he was pierced for our transgressions; he was crushed for our iniquities; upon him was the chastisement that brought us peace, and with his wounds we are healed.

Isaiah 53:5

The Inexplicable

Many events occur in which there appears to be no answer to the question, "Why?"

When a tsunami kills thousands.

When a tornado destroys an elementary school in Oklahoma, killing children, why?

When a city bus driver goes into insulin shock, passing out at the wheel, driving into an oncoming car, and killing the occupant inside.

When all those little kiddos with cancer enter St. Jude's Children's Hospital. Thank goodness for those wonderful people at St. Jude's!

From my years in South Africa, the countless abused, violated, sick children, dying with seemingly no one to help them.

I want to think God cares and has a plan for all of this. That's what faith is about, I guess. But in the areas I don't understand, it's not very easy—I admit this. How can we come to any conclusions about God in such matters?

Philip Yancey words are worth consideration:

We may experience times of unusual closeness, when every prayer is answered in an obvious way and God seems intimate and caring.

And we may also experience 'fog times' when God stays silent when nothing works according to formula, and all the Bible's promises seem glaringly false.

156

Fidelity involves learning to trust that, out beyond the perimeter of fog, God still reigns and has not abandoned us, no matter how it appears.[92]

Let God Into Your Pain

I think we sometimes lock God out of our hurts. Maybe it's because we don't feel God particularly interests himself in our aches. Or that we're unworthy of God's time.

We unknowingly become Christian agnostics, struggling with the pain of our pasts.

When we allow God into our pain instead of ruminating about what we don't understand, pain can become purposeful. At least, that's the way it works for me.

Paul dealt with a painful personal issue. He went to God three times about it.

Each time he said, 'My grace is all you need. My power works best in weakness.'

So now I am glad to boast about my weaknesses, so that the power of Christ can work through me.
That's why I take pleasure in my weaknesses, and in the insults, hardships, persecutions, and troubles that I suffer for Christ. For when I am weak, then I am strong.

2 Corinthians 12:9b-10

When God refused to remove his pain, he came to three conclusions about:

1. God's Promise

Remember, I am here for you. My grace—favor, and presence—is enough to guide you through this. In me, you're an overcomer!

What weakens you can strengthen you. Your struggles are not purposeless; they build strength and resilience to bring you closer to ME.

God's promises are unwavering. He will never leave or forsake us, never walk away, and never leave us stranded in our pasts.

I will never fail you. I will never abandon you

Hebrew 13:5, Isaiah 41:10

When we walk through our Valleys of the Shadow of Death, the Great Shepherd accompanies us. Psalm 23

2. God's Presence

Remember, God is just as much a part of our pasts as we are. Theologically, we know God is everywhere. However, it's sometimes a struggle to sense God's presence in our long ago. But take heart, for He was there, even in the most challenging of moments.

We can take negative, harmful thoughts captive, making them prisoners, gaining control over our thinking process.

We demolish arguments and every pretension that sets itself up against the knowledge of God, and we take captive every thought to make it obedient to Christ.

2 Corinthians 10:5 NIV

3. God's Purpose

From my past, as troublesome as it was, I can now see God in it. While painful at the moment of impact, a troubled past can move us toward a meaningful purpose.

Upon finding purpose in pain, pain becomes tolerable. And pain can also become productive.

He comforts us in all our troubles <u>so</u> <u>that</u> <u>we</u> <u>can</u> <u>comfort</u> <u>others</u>. When they are troubled, we will be able to give them the same comfort God has given us.

2 Corinthians 1:4

Moving Forward

Acknowledge the pain of your past. It's what makes you, you. The past is part of your present. Manage it in the light of God's Word and healing care. With God, your past can aid you in moving toward a better future.

You go before me and follow me.
You place your hand of blessing on my head.

Every day of my life was recorded in your book.
Every moment was laid out before
a single day had passed.

And when I wake up, you are still with me!

Psalm 139:5, 16, 18b

Incessant
Illnesses

IF YOU'RE A MEMBER OF the Missionary Chronic Illness Club, welcome. I've been part of this happy group for many years now.

It wasn't until I was diagnosed with FSH Muscular Dystrophy at the age of sixty-two that empathy for my youngest brother Robert went from feeling bad for the guy to, "How did he deal with this for his sixty-one years of life?"

I used to wonder why he often dressed so slovenly. Usually, he'd appear in oversized sweatpants and a giant baggy sweatshirt, unshaven and unkempt.

Now, I get it. Getting up, showering, grooming, and dressing are often the biggest challenges of my day. They're painful, leaving me exhausted and frequently agitated. Thankfully, Kathy is there to help me.

Robert considered me a good brother, telling me a hundred times that he loved me. But I wish I could be there again, to do it all over with the camaraderie we'd now share.

He's been gone for over a year now. I'm just beginning this long, muscle-wasting, embarrassing, humiliating, painful, and debilitating journey, which guarantees continual pain and loss of upper body strength. I hurt for him. I hurt for me. I hurt for you, too, my missionary friend.

I wish I had the power to remove your monster disorder, which, on the best of days, like a toothache, reminds you, "You'll never be rid of me," and on the worst of days, stands over you in ridicule, mocking, "Ready for your beating today?" Like Gandalf in the underground realm of Moria,[93] I'd deliver you from your menacing Balrog[94].

But I don't possess such a staff or wield that kind of power. So all I can do is say,

I'm so very, very sorry this happened to you. I hurt with you and for you. Life is often difficult, especially for those of us who've given our lives for the Gospel's sake and seemingly, at times, received a curse rather than thanks for our efforts. But God is faithful, especially in our pain, and that 'curse' can take on the face of a comforter to others.

 Often, we minister and serve with a limp. Sometimes, we hide behind a smile because it's necessary. And no one wants to listen to someone extol pain, emotional duress, and misery about their malaises.

Here's what I've learned. Many become uncomfortable when I talk about my Muscular Dystrophy or my PTSD. They can't relate, feel helpless to do anything about it, and tend to avoid me when I do so.

So, I smile or try to anyway.

Louis Armstrong and Frank Sinatra made the song *When You're Smiling* popular. Remember how it goes?

When you're smilin'
When you're smilin'
The whole world smiles with you…

There's a bit of truth there. A smile often puts people at ease. Even in pain, we can learn to smile. As chronic pain sufferers, we, as missionaries, need to develop this discipline, if only for the sake of others. However, sometimes we can't hide our pain, anxiety, or downhearted spirit. Can we?

Yeah… I know about "Casting all your anxiety upon him for…" My theology knows this is true, but my heart sometimes struggles to connect.

Ever feel that way?

My life is a chronic pain trainwreck, and it's only getting worse. I've looked at many options for dealing with it. Then, there's depression and anxiety that comes with it too.

Most of all, it hinders me from involving myself in activities I once enjoyed and causes me to feel embarrassed around people sometimes.

It often angers me as well, although I've learned to hide this around people.

I stopped going to Men's Prayer Breakfast a while back because the difficulty of putting food on my plate and carrying it back to the table mortified me. There's a 50-50 chance I'll spill my coffee or juice if I can even get it to the table in the first place.

So, I thought I'd come to the Men's Prayer Breakfast, and after prayer, when all the guys got up to go through the buffet line, I'd remain seated at the table.

If asked why I had not eaten, I'd respond that I'd already eaten at home, really only consuming a donut with a cup of coffee on the drive to church.

So….there I was one Saturday morning, sitting after the blessing as fifty men began to get into line.

But a friend came alongside me and asked, "Hey, can I get you some breakfast?"

God is good, and so are most of His people. I'm thankful.

Dealing With Chronic Pain and Illness

Again, please understand. I am neither a physician nor possess formal training or certification in pain management, pharmacology, or mental health care. What I am is a missionary who's dealt with my own chronic pain and mental health for years. Here, I share my discoveries, experiences, thoughts, and advice.

Please do not change your current health practices without consulting your doctor, therapist, or mental health professional first.

How do we handle chronic pain? I mean, how can one function consistently in discomfort and hurt? What do you do when the apparent becomes evident: this ain't never going away?

We do the best we can. No miracle answers here. No matter how you cut it, it's unfair, not right, but still a part of every moment of our lives. It just plain sucks.

We, as missionaries, are particularly susceptible because of the environments we expose ourselves to—environments that no pastor, missions trip vacationer, or traveling businessperson will ever understand.

Recently, I spoke with a missionary who's experienced thirteen bouts of malaria. Another spoke of a brain infection contracted in a third-world environment, an infection that is uncurable.

While I don't know everything here or purport to understand what you're going through, I share thoughts from a fellow combatant. May it offer you comfort and help.

Types of Pain

There are two main types of pain:[95]

- Acute Pain – a normal response to an injury or medical condition. It starts suddenly and is usually short-lived.

- Chronic Pain – continues beyond the time expected for healing. It generally lasts longer than three months.

"Pain may be anything from a dull ache to a sharp stab. It ranges from mild to extreme. You may feel pain in one part of your body, or it may be widespread."[96]

What to Do?

Ted Jones, PhD lists 5 Coping Skills Every Chronic Pain Patient Needs to Understand and Master:[97]

- **Understanding** – learn all you can about your condition. Make yourself aware of the possibilities. Listen to the experts. Let them become your coaches about:

  o Your exercise, physical & occupational therapy.
  o Medications – benefits and limitations. Become knowledgeable of their interactions with other meds you're taking. Follow the instructions for taking your meds.
  o Mental health – chronic pain and debilitating conditions wear you down, producing a host of mental health issues. I'm not in the 'Christian' camp that believes therapists, therapies, and medications that improve mental health are a sin or lack of trust in God.
  o Don't wait until debilitation becomes your mantra.

Yet, missionaries, we put off the inevitable, don't we? I don't know the number of missionaries who won't see a health professional until nearly reaching a debilitated state, let alone follow their advice. Gain as much understanding about your condition as possible. I can almost give a lecture about Facioscapulohumeral Muscular Dystrophy.

- **Accepting** – often, when learning of a serious ailment, the first reaction is disbelief. With some, they catastrophize their diagnosis, imagining the worst outcome possible.

For me, it was denial. Putting off seeing a doctor until I could no longer put off seeing a doctor. It became this critical, see a doctor or die. Then disbelief and anger entered the equation.

The sooner we accept our new reality, the sooner we can navigate life as we learn to deal with our CPS, Chronic Pain Syndrome.

Be Careful of the 'I Should Be's'

- I should be a person of more faith, then this would disappear.
- I should be able to help my family more.
- I should be able to lift my newborn grandbaby to cuddle and hold. But I can't.
- I should be able to work a full-time job.
- I should be more spiritual at this.
- I should be able to report to all my supporters.
- I should be able to stay in that crummy missionary apartment, again.
- I should be able to raise more support.
- I should be able to eliminate this pain by prayer, aromatherapy, blue-green algae, vitamins, drug therapy, and, and, and…
- I should be able to not let pain get to me like this.
- I should be able to deal with this pain without medication.

- I should be able to attend every service, conference, and duty, even though I'm barely functional at times.
- I should be able to play guitar as well as I used to.
- For me, too, I should be able to golf, fish—I love fishing—hunt, and drive my pontoon boat—gave that away last year—along with my golf clubs, fishing gear, and, and, …
- I should still be able to drive 6,000 miles a month, reporting to my supporters.
- I should be able to trust God more. Yes, true, but guilt rarely accomplishes this.
- I should be able to smile all the time when around people, even though I'm tormented with pain and struggling with depression, and IT TOOK ME ALMOST TWO HOURS TO SHOWER AND GET DRESSED THIS MORNING!
- I should be able to button my own shirt.
- I should, I should, I should…

My son Daniel encouraged me to stop thinking, "I should be able." He said, "Dad, celebrate; I can."

I can write today.
I can publish another book to encourage missionaries.
I can still play bass or guitar on the worship team, though that ability is slipping away.
I can still drive.
I can still hug my Kathy.
I can still visit my grandkidos.
I can, I can, I can!

He said, "Dad, Muscular Dystrophy doesn't affect your brain, ability to articulate, or heart for life and helping people. And Dad, don't let Muscular Dystrophy define you. You define yourself. Dad, celebrate what you can do…not continually repeat what you can no longer do."

166

Good stuff there. Don't you think? This is spoken by an individual who's suffered from chronic pain every day of his life due to Still's disease.

- **Calming** – Dr. Ted Jones notes:

Pain is meant to stimulate the body into action and avoid danger. This is the well-known "fight or flight" response. The natural reaction of patients with pain is to be in continual physiological arousal.

The problem is that because the pain is ongoing, stress can be augmented by it. Therefore, learning how to calm the body down is an essential skill for managing pain.

Diaphragmatic breathing can help calm the body down. When in pain, we tend to tighten up or clench, considerably reducing our ability to breathe in oxygen. Search YouTube for countless examples of this technique.[98]

The YouVersion Bible App often encourages diaphragmatic breathing in its daily guided Scripture devotional under *Cultivate a Rhythm of Reflection.*

- **Balancing.** Dr. Jones states, "This skill is a collection of various techniques and skills that revolve around creating a balanced and sustainable lifestyle."[99]

Here's the big one: it's the whole enchilada.

It's called '**activity pacing**.' It's the process of learning not to overdo it while staying active.[100]

My journey with 'activity pacing' began when I heard the advice of a friend who also has FSH Muscular Dystrophy. His words resonated with me and became the starting point of my own activity pacing strategy.

He said, "Don, it's all about energy conservation—not overdoing it. You've only got so much energy at the beginning of each day. Far less than almost everyone else you know.

You'll discover that overdoing it occurs within shorter periods. It won't take much to fatigue you. Your biggest challenge is figuring out how and when to use your limited energy supply."

He finished, "And my friend, stubbornness is not your friend."

It doesn't mean you can't do life or ministry! It means you'll need to develop a keen situational awareness of your limits.

Often, I'm completely exhausted and in bed by 8:00 pm. When in evening meetings, forced sleep is required in the afternoon, or like the tortoise and the hare, I'll finish last.

Learn to manage your condition, or it will manage you. Believe me, you don't want to be on the last part of that sentence. Be master of your pain. Make pain serve you rather than allow chronic aches and illness to enslave you.

- **Coping**. Dr. Jones comments, "The final skill is coping—that is, having tips, techniques, and plans to use when the pain becomes more severe."[101]

That is why I personally utilize professional psychology. My therapists train and enable me with skills and techniques to manage my pain and PTSD.

Again, I want to manage my condition rather than it manage me. I will take control of my body, mind, and spirit rather than allow it to control me.

Pain, constant illness, and debilitating health conditions warrant a variety of different approaches. Hurt can beat the stuffings out of a person as it intensifies. I try to stay ahead of my pain.

Acetaminophen, naproxen, aspirin, analgesic ointments, and other OTC (over-the-counter) medications can lower pain levels and calm chronic illness.

A word of caution here. Over-the-counter drugs provide excellent pain relief benefits, but they also carry significant side effects, mainly when used in excess.

I had a friend who, after a botched surgical procedure, found herself in immense pain. On the pain scale of 1 to 10, she lived every day between 7-10. To help take the edge off, she existed on a steady diet of liquid acetaminophen apart from her doctor's knowledge. She bought the stuff by the gallon.

Three years after her surgery, she died of kidney complications as a direct result of her acetaminophen consumption.

When purchasing OTC drugs, it is a good idea to gain as much knowledge as possible about the medicines you are buying.

In the beginning, my consumption of OTC drugs helped produce analgesia or a state of being both conscious and pain-free.

After a few years, as this disease forced my muscles into continual wasting atrophy, the pain intensified. I knew what was coming as I'd watched my little brother deal with the disease for fifty years.

My pain management entered a new stage of medication treatment. Severe chronic pain is often treated periodically with opioids. The opioid crisis of the past two decades has some believing no valid reason exists for taking opioids. This is not the case.

I'm cautious with my medications. Once a quarter, I meet with my doctor to discuss those medications and adjust them as needed.

One day, stronger pain meds will become necessary for me as this MD demon continues to lay waste to my body, but a drug addiction added to everything else is the last thing I need or want. Therefore, attentiveness is essential.

Don't be duped into an addiction. For chronic pain sufferers, it's an easy hole to fall into.

Another thing. Cross-reference all medications, whether aspirin, Tylenol, Aleve, or prescription drugs, in a search to identify harmful interactions between prescription drugs and OTC drugs. WebMD is beneficial. Here is a synopsis of their suggestions:[102]

Two or more drugs that share the same active ingredient can become a severe health problem. For example:

Be careful when taking blood-thinning drugs with NSAIDs. NSAIDS—nonsteroidal anti-inflammatory drugs—or pain relievers like ibuprofen and naproxen. If you're on a blood thinner, ask your doctor to suggest a different type of over-the-counter pain medication and dose that's safe for you.

Pills with antihistamines can cause you to react more slowly, making it dangerous to drive or use heavy machinery.

Taking a standard OTC of omeprazole for acid reflux relief when mixed with a thyroid drug called levothyroxine can be dangerous.

SSRIs, Serotonin Selective Uptake Inhibitors, commonly used in mental health to treat depression, if taken with another medicine that affects serotonin like Tramadol, Trazadone, or Linezolid, can result in "serotonin syndrome, characterized by neuromuscular irritation, autonomic nervous system excitation, and altered mental state."[103]

Foods Can Adversely Affect Drugs

Too much grapefruit or grapefruit juice can affect drugs like Statins, Antihistamines, Blood pressure drugs, anxiety meds, or transplant antirejection drugs.

Foods with vitamin K, like leafy greens, can interact with the blood thinner warfarin. You don't have to stop eating them, but it's essential to be consistent and not overdo it. Ask your doctor how much food with vitamin K you can consume, and then eat the same amount around the same time each day.[104]

High-potassium foods and drinks, like bananas, salt substitutes, and orange juice, can affect blood ACE inhibitors.[105]

It's crucial to always consult with your doctor or pharmacist before considering any supplements. This is a standard practice that ensures your health and safety. My doctors always ask, "What supplements are you taking?"

Drinking alcohol with some medications carries a host of adverse effects. Here, many tend to ignore this. Yet, a few years back, I performed a funeral for a beautiful young woman, a mother of two, who drank alcohol while taking a double dose of prescribed medication.

Avoid Negative Drug Interactions

Read labels carefully. Most drug labels or patient handouts don't list every possible drug interaction.

Pharmacists are experts on medicine safety. Use their expertise to ensure a safe medication experience.

Work closely with your doctors. **Make sure** they possess a list of every medication you're currently taking. Don't assume your doctors know what each other is prescribing you. And...don't cross-pollinate between doctors to obtain drugs other than for prescribed medical reasons.[106]

Missionaries, I'm talking with us here. We've seen this several times over the decades: a missionary either not informing doctors of their meds or deliberately gaming the system to abuse medications.

No shame here. Just trying to help us all live healthier lives. We, as missionaries, suffer from a variety of disorders and illnesses, from cancer, kidney disease, malaria, dengue fever, and bilharzia to autoimmune diseases, to name a few. Learning to manage your condition is everything.

I suggest following a pain management approach in treating chronic pain and illness.

The 5 A's of Pain Management in the National Library of Medicine from the Ochsner Journal,[107] here, simplified by the Pain Outlet Clinical Guide, are:[108]

Analgesia

- To what extent has pain been reduced to the acceptable negotiated level? In other words, pain you can live with.*

Activities of Daily Living

- The extent to which **work, play, and socialization** are positively or negatively impacted by pain **or** analgesic regimen. How does your daily activity affect your pain level or your medications?

Adverse Effects

- The extent to which **adverse effects** of analgesic regimens and medications are minimized.

Aberrant Drug-related Behaviors

- Evidence for drug **addiction** or drug ****diversion**.

Affect

- The extent to which **mood and sleep** have been positively or negatively impacted by pain **or** analgesic regimen.

* The process of making a bad or unpleasant situation better: Regular exercise can provide gradual amelioration of anxiety. Example: treatment for her allergies led to the amelioration of her symptoms.[109]

** Drug diversion is the illegal distribution or abuse of prescription drugs or their use for purposes not intended by the prescriber.[110]

Pain Management Strategies

A typical pain management strategy when chronic pain is unbearable:[111]

- Pain medicines.
- Physical therapies including heat or cold packs, massage, hydrotherapy, and exercise.
- Psychological therapies—cognitive behavioral therapy, relaxation techniques, and meditation.
- Mind and body techniques—such as acupuncture.
- Community support groups.

Medical health professionals often employ this model. It helped me understand health professionals' approach to dealing with my condition. I can politely accept or reject an approach or proposal I dislike here. The Mayo Clinic offers some additional excellent advice for coping strategies:[112]

Practice Breathing Exercises

Inhale slowly through the nose, allow your lungs and belly to expand, hold for four seconds, and then exhale slowly through your mouth and nose. Hold again for four seconds, and then breathe in. Repeat often throughout the day.

Get Moving

Work with a physical or occupational therapist on appropriate exercises to gradually retrain your body.
Incorporate a gentle stretching program, such as yoga or tai chi, for added comfort and safety into your routine.

These activities are designed to be gentle on your body, making them ideal for pain management. Most importantly, get moving, but be smart about it.

Participate in Meaningful Activities

Exercise activates the body's natural, feel-good chemicals called endorphins. Set aside time each day for a simple activity that is calming or brings you joy.

Engage in Mindfulness

Meditation, at its core, is a simple practice. It's about being in the present moment, free from any interpretation or judgment. To start, you can focus on one sensory input at a time, like the sound of your breath or the feeling of your body against a surface.

Christian music, which I repeatedly play on the guitar, coursing through my mind, focuses my mental acuity.

Use Moderation and Pacing

Set realistic goals and start by doing one-third of what you think you can do. Try setting a timer to remind yourself to take a break for more complex tasks.

Practice Good Sleep Habits

Establishing consistent bed and wake times is crucial. This practice helps regulate your body's internal clock, making it easier to you to fall asleep and wake up at the desired times. Remember, your bed is for sleep, not spending your entire day there.

Don't stay up watching TV until you slip off into a coma. Or stare at your phone, scrolling through Facebook, Instagram, or TikTok reels. These activities have a way of fooling your brain into alertness when, in fact, your body is screaming for sleep.

Eliminate Unhelpful Substances

Smoking restricts blood flow, which prevents healing. Alcohol creates nerve damage over time.

I knew a missionary who consumed 4 liters of Diet Coke a day. Need I say more?

Treat Related Conditions

Cognitive behavioral therapy with a licensed mental health professional helps decrease symptoms of depression, anxiety, and other psychological and physical health concerns.

Stay Connected to Your Support System

While taking time for yourself is crucial, having family and friends who care about you is essential. Although you may want to be left alone during bouts of chronic pain and illness, lean into them for support.

Up till now, I've left the spiritual dynamics of dealing with chronic pain and illness out of the equation. *This is the essence of setting sail and staying on course in a meaningful journey during pain's continual tempests.*

Dealing with our maladies spiritually becomes the most essential part of handling them. We must see God in the equation...because God is the master of our equation, and without him, everything becomes meaningless.

> *We must see God in the equation.*

That Thorn in the Flesh

In 2 Corinthians 12:7-10, Paul discusses the life-altering thorn in his flesh that affected and changed his life, as mentioned in the previous pages. No one knows what that thorn was precisely, but Scripture indicates that he perhaps suffered from a severe eye affliction.

After visiting the Galatia church, Paul felt compelled to extend his guidance and support. This led to the creation of a follow-up letter:

175

Surely you remember that I was sick when I first brought you the Good News.

But even though my condition tempted you to reject me, you did not despise me or turn me away. No, you took me in and cared for me as though I were an angel from God or even Christ Jesus himself.

Where is that joyful and grateful spirit you felt then? I am sure you would have **taken out your own eyes and given them to me** if it had been possible.

Galatians 4:13-15

Toward the end of the letter, he finishes by acknowledging that his handwriting was recognizable because of the large letters he made:

See what large letters I use as I write to you with my own hand!

Galatians 6:11 NIV

Furthermore, he was temporality blinded in Acts 9:8. When his sight was restored, it's vividly described in a moment of divine intervention, "Instantly something like scales fell from Saul's eyes, and he regained his sight. Then he got up and was baptized." Acts 9:18

Later, he fails to recognize the high priest when appearing before the Jewish council in Jerusalem:

Those standing near Paul said to him, 'Do you dare to insult God's high priest?'

'I'm sorry, brothers. I didn't realize he was the high priest,' Paul replied, for the Scriptures say, 'You must not speak evil of any of your rulers.'

Acts 23:4-5

As many times as Paul experienced beatings, stoning, whippings, shipwrecks, and other extreme experiences, it's not far-fetched to say Paul suffered from horrific chronic pain and physical deformities.

Who knows whether this resulted in Paul's Thorn in the Flesh? But whatever it was, it produced an unwanted chronic condition, whether spiritual, emotional, or physical—perhaps all three. Paul learned to deal with his tormentor. What did he do?

First, Paul Considered Pain's Benefits:

So to keep me from becoming proud, I was given a thorn in my flesh, a messenger from Satan to torment me and **keep me from becoming proud.**

2 Corinthians 12:7

This is a biggy, my friends. Suppose your pain seems purposeless and senseless, an inexplicable result of fate, back luck, or whatever. In that case, you'll sit listless in life's winds, unable to catch any momentum into your sails as the gales of pain or illness drive you into the rocks of despair.

You drive your pain. Don't allow it to drive you.

Next, Paul put God in the Equation

Three different times I begged the Lord to take it away.

12 Corinthians 12:8

Reminds me of Jesus words:

And so I tell you, keep on asking, and you will receive what you ask for. Keep on seeking, and you will find. Keep on knocking, and the door will be opened to you. [10] For everyone

177

who asks, receives. Everyone who seeks, finds. And to everyone who knocks, the door will be opened.

Luke 11:9-11

Paul Discovered an Answer to His Prayer

"Each time he said, '*My grace is all you need.* My power
works best in weakness.'"

2 Corinthians 12:9a

Let's consider a few questions:

For Christ's followers, are our lives driven by accidents, misfor-
tunes, or fate?

Maybe it's all just a crapshoot?

Or… perhaps purpose exists in our pain as a means to draw us
closer to God, and nearer to people with more empathy and identification with Christ. Weakness can focus our attention away from ourselves and towards God with a willingness to help others.

Purpose in Pain

My power works best in weakness... that the power of Christ
can work through me. *For when I am weak, then I am strong.*

2 Corinthians 12:9a & 10b

Beneficial Results?

So now I am glad to boast about my weaknesses, so that the
power of Christ can work through me.

That's why I take pleasure in my *weaknesses,* and in the *insults, hardships, persecutions,* and *troubles* that I suffer for
Christ.

2 Corinthians 12:9b-10a

If you could see every event in your life as potentially bringing you closer to a Christlike attitude and response, wouldn't that offer hope in coping with your troubles and afflictions?

Father, bless my friends reading these words. Whatever the situation, problem, illness, or hardship, help them see You. We know everything works for good, but we often struggle to grasp hold of this truth. May they actively seek Your presence in their lives.

We know you heal for your purpose and glory, but you don't heal everyone who asks. And none of us escape that ultimate sickness: death.

Pain overwhelms us at times, cutting down our ability and desire to want you in our lives. Your presence can seem far away when pain and sorrow bear upon us.

So, please help us sense your presence and see it through the lens of your son, who hung on that cross so long ago, experiencing every pain and challenge we face. In his understanding, we find comfort.

Help us see Jesus, for by his stripes, we are healed.

Amen, and Amen.

The LORD sustains them on their sickbed and restores them from their bed of illness.

Psalm 41:3 NIV

Sin
Struggles

OK. LET'S BEGIN A TRANSPARENT CONVERSATION HERE. We missionaries, all of us, struggle with sin issues. Don't we?

Luke[113] put it this way:

> Therefore, since we are surrounded by such a great cloud of witnesses, let us throw off *everything* that **hinders** and ***the sin*** *that so easily* <u>*entangles*</u>. And let us run with perseverance the race marked out for us...

> Hebrews 12:1 NIV

Notice the word we in which the writer of Hebrews includes himself. He admonishes every follower of Christ, assuming we all struggle with sin. Sin deters us from running the race marked out for us by God.

We all struggle with sin issues.

The cloud of witnesses is all those people mentioned in Hebrews chapter eleven. These examples encourage us to rid ourselves of any sin that hinders, sidetracks, or distracts us.

'Let us' refers to Hebrew Christian believers who had professed Christ but had not yet reached spiritual maturity or fallen back in their faith.[114]

And '...*the sin that so easily entangles*', in Greek, literally means "*sin that* easily <u>stands</u> around us."[115]

That sin that 'stands around' us. Hum… sin always hangs around us. Doesn't it?

'Entangles' is also translated as hinders, cling unto, weighs down, obstacle, encumbrance, or anything that slows you down.

Question: What is that one thing in your life that trips you up? Slows you down? Sidetracks you? Hinders you? Like an unwelcome parasitic guest, it lives in a symbiont relationship within your soul. It's always standing around you.

You spread out our sins before you—our **secret** **sins**—and <u>you</u> <u>see</u> <u>them</u> <u>all</u>.

Psalm 90:8

 Ask God to show you… if… uncertain. Sinful leanings that we don't see as an issue in our lives or what we hide from ourselves and others.

King David asked, "Keep your servant from deliberate sins! Don't let them control me. Then I will be free of guilt and innocent of great sin." Psalm 19:13

"To be free…" is the aim. To be unrestricted of anything that might slow you down, trip you up, hinder you, or prevent you from ripening to your full potential in life and faith.

The imagery is that of an athlete who would strip every bit of clothing off that might weigh them down from competing well in a race.[116]

Just what is that weight of hindrance in your life, hiding behind your smile? That one thing pushing you off course? Keepin you out of the race? It may seem minor to others, but it's a big, hairy deal for you.

That fear of…

182

That bitterness towards…
The worry of…
That anger with…
Doubt about…
Deception of…
Lusting towards…
Poisoned viewing…
The temptation always standing around…
Cravings of…
Weighs you down…
Stifles your faith…
Apathy about…
Secrets of…
Envying…
Coveting that one thing above all else…
Discontentment about…

What is it? *Your Achilles Heel of sin-leanings?* Like a laser-guided missile, focus yourself on the sinful spot in your life that weighs you down.

I'm weighed down by: _____.

Once, while on the massive Lake of the Woods, my phone died, leaving me without GPS to return to our destination.

The massive 951,000-acre lake is over 70 miles long and wide. From the distance, we couldn't see the shoreline. And while I knew the direction from where we came, visually, my line of sight to return was somewhat precarious.

The lake contains thousands of islands. I paid attention to each one we passed on the journey to the middle of the lake, especially the last one. So, I set my sights on it. Once I reached that island passing by, I fixed my eyes on the next island. Following one after another, finally, in the distance, stood a tower behind the boat launch where we'd begun our journey.

Fixing my eye from point to point brought us safely back from a risky situation. In like manner, fix our souls from point to point upon Jesus, the Way, Truth, and Life.

What do you fix your spiritual eyes—thoughts, emotions, and focus—upon? Whatever, whoever, or wherever that fixation gazes, becomes the determiner of the treasures of your heart. "For where your treasure is, there your heart will be also." —Jesus Matthew 6:21 KJV

Looking Unto Jesus

Once, in the midst of a heart-wrenching tragedy, I shared a verse from the Bible with a missionary. He blurted out, "But why?" I know what this verse says. I know the truth of it, but my heart screams out, 'Why should I look to Jesus after all the losses we've suffered.'"

Then, his head dropped, his eyes looked to the floor, and he continued, "I know. That's very unspiritual of me."

Who among us has not reflected a similar thought in our lowest moments?

So, we went to the same Scriptures in Hebrews 12:1-2, and the answer to 'why' welcomed us.

...let us lay aside every weight, and the sin which doth so easily beset us, and let us run with patience the race that is set before us...

Looking unto Jesus the author and finisher of our faith...

The King James version of Hebrews 12 begins with "Looking..." This word is translated from the Greek word *aphoraō* and implies "to look away from one thing to see another, to concentrate the gaze upon."

It means *"Looking from afar."*[117] We find the same Greek word in 'I shall see,' Philippians 2:23:

> Him therefore I hope to send presently, so soon as I <u>shall</u> <u>see</u> how it will go with me. KJV

This word, *aphoraō,* occurs only two times in the New Testament. In Hebrews 12:2, 'looking' and here, in Philippians 2:23 with 'I shall see.' [118]

Now, back to the question of, 'Why?' Why should we continuously look to Jesus, especially in our most challenging and darkest times? The words and verses in Hebrews 12:2-3 reassure us:

We do this by **keeping our eyes on Jesus**, the [a]champion who [b]initiates and perfects our faith.

Because of the [d]joy awaiting him, **he endured the cross**, [c]disregarding its shame. Now he is seated in the **place of honor** beside God's throne.

Think of all the hostility he endured from sinful people; [e]then you won't become weary and give up.

Jesus our [a]Champion

He's the Author, 'Prince Leader,' the 'Captain' of our salvation. He goes before us as the Originator of our faith whose matchless example we need always follow.[119]

Jesus, then, is the rightful owner of my salvation—a redemption he purchased on Calvary. He grants this salvation upon my pledge of faith in his person.

185

If Jesus is the Captain, who better than to skipper my soul through these troublesome waters of this life?[120]

Jesus, the Initiator, [b]Perfecting our Faith

Jesus conquered death on the cross, atoning—covering over our sins. Only he, the Initiator, Pioneer, and Founder, can guide our faith to its final destination. Jesus stands before us as faith's highest value; Himself.

Disregarding the [c]Shame of the Cross

The ancient world's cross was reserved for the worst of the worst. Only the lowest of the human element went to death's cross.

Crucifixion was more than pain and punishment. It sought absolute humiliation. It was thought of as the most horrible, painful, tortuous, and humiliating form of execution possible.[121]

Convicted cross-criminals became spectacles of mocking, spitting, and swearing crowds. Most of the convicted were hung, tormented, and naked.[122]

Upon the crucified's death, the final degradation and shame came when bodies were left on the cross to decompose subject to scavenging animals.[123]

Finally, crucifixion announced a warning to all others who might oppose the Roman government and its laws. Why, then, did Jesus agree to such a horrendous physical ending?

[d]The Cross Overshadows Shame

Oh, what joy for those whose disobedience is forgiven, whose sins are put out of sight. Yes, what joy for those whose record the Lord has cleared of sin. Romans 4:7-8

What joy? Being seated beside God! Not only joy but a pardon granting us, you and me, payment and releasing us from our sins. Jesus suffered the shame of the cross to redeem us and make us valuable again. The final result?

[e]Keeps Us From Giving Up

So let's <u>not</u> <u>get</u> <u>tired</u> of doing what is good. At just the right time we will reap a harvest of blessing <u>if</u> <u>we</u> <u>don't</u> <u>give</u> <u>up</u>.

Galatians 6:9

How about it? Will you place any sin struggles in the shadow of that beautiful cross of Jesus? After all:

We know that <u>our</u> <u>old</u> <u>sinful</u> <u>selves</u> <u>were</u> <u>crucified</u> <u>with</u> <u>Christ</u> so that *sin might lose its power in our lives.* **We are no longer slaves** to sin. For when we died with Christ <u>we</u> <u>were</u> <u>set</u> <u>free</u> from the power of sin. And since we died with Christ, *we know we will also live with him.*

Romans 6:6-8

He has removed our sins as far from us
as the east is from the west.

Psalm 103:12

My Soul Smile

If I say, 'I will forget my complaint, I will
change my expression, and smile,'
I still dread...

Job 9:27 NIV

LOOK, MISSIONARY LIFE IS DEMANDING. *Behind the Missionary Smile* reminds me of the old song *Smile*.

Smile though your heart is aching
Smile even though it's breaking
When there are clouds in the sky
You'll get by...

It's sort of how missionary life works sometimes. From time to time, we must smile regardless. Yet, when our outward smile becomes the only smile of our spiritual dispositions, we're in trouble.

Like Job, "If I forget my complaints, put away my sad face, and become cheerful, I'd still dread..."

There are a lot of dreading missionaries out there. Too often, we eke out our demanding missionary existence by 'just grin and bear it.' And like the song above says, "You'll get by..."

But that's all you'll do: get by.

Missionaries living in a just-get-by mode easily stand out in stark contrast to the abundant life we claim to represent in Jesus. There's little margin for anything else when we're just getting by.

In this, we try to survive on trifled grins while fundraising, reporting, and representing, projecting a smile through undernourished souls.

My many years with those wonderful African people in Zululand, South Africa, testified to the energy and intensity of living in a just-get-by manner.

Every moment of their energy's existence went towards acquiring the pittance upon which they were expected to survive. People on bare subsistence showed signs of malnutrition, underdevelopment, and desperation.

Yet, the equation changed when Jesus entered that barren existence. Jesus' joy marked their new life. Yes, like Job, pain still made up a share of life's equation as it does for many, but Jesus changed their outlook.

They could look beyond their pain and smile. They discovered the truth behind Christ's promise…life beyond this life.

I am come that they **might have life**, and that they might have *it* more abundantly.

— Jesus John 10:10 KJV

Our inner smile originates from the Abundant Life in Christ. I like to call this *__my soul-smile__*. A soul smile that looks past the happenings of this life and reflects Christ's words,

My sheep listen to my voice; I know them, and they follow me. **I give them eternal life**, and they will never perish. No one can snatch them away from me…"

John 10:27-28

189

Your Soul Smile

Even though your heart is aching, even though it's breaking, and even when the challenges of missionary life mount to overwhelming proportions, focus on Jesus. Here's the essence of a soul smile:

Anyone who believes in me may come and drink! For the Scriptures declare, 'Rivers of living water will flow from his heart.'

Jesus ~ John 7:38

Watching rippling river waters alongside lush green grass-covered banks reflects a smiling disposition within me. Now, my muscular pain may excruciate me, but when looking at a clean, beautiful Minnesota lake, I can still smile even though FSH Muscular Dystrophy is crucifying me.

When a slamming door tears a strip off my TBI brain, my soul can smile even though:

Oh, what a miserable person I am! <u>Who</u> <u>will</u> <u>free</u> <u>me</u> <u>from</u> <u>this</u> <u>life</u> that is dominated by sin and death? Thank God! The answer is in **Jesus Christ our Lord**.

Romans 7:24-25a

Placing faith in Jesus provides a spiritual dynamic in the renewal of life through the transformative power of Jesus Christ.[124]

My soul smiles.

Do not let your hearts be troubled... I am going to prepare a place for you; I will come and get you...

John 14:1a, 2b, 3a

My soul smiles.

Jesus transcends the just-getting-by smiles of our flesh with the hope encapsulated in him.

My soul smiles.

Our life in Jesus is not simply a state of existence but a source of joy that defies this world's understanding. It starkly contrasts with the emptiness and dissatisfaction bombarding us today.

My soul smiles.

In Jesus, we discover a life that is not solely governed by our emotions, station in life, successes or failures, hardships, and pleasures but also overflows with the richness of Jesus Christ. Let us live with the hope that he is preparing that special place. John 14:1-4

Our souls can smile because:

Life in Christ gives us assurance before, now, then, and after.

Our souls can smile because God loves us. Jesus Christ proves it!

So, my friend, let your soul smile in the promise of Christ:

> *I tell you the truth, those who listen to my message and believe in God who sent me have eternal life.*
> *They will never be condemned for their sins,*
> *but they have already passed from death into life.*
>
> *John 5:24*

About the Author

Don and his wife Kathy served as missionaries in South Africa for twenty-two years. He then pastored two churches in Minnesota. Currently, Don and Kathy serve in Member Care for missionaries and pastors worldwide.

Don holds a bachelor's degree from Baptist Bible College in Springfield, Missouri, a master's degree in theology from Bethany Theological Seminary in Dothan, Alabama, and a Master's and Doctor of Ministry from Luther Rice Seminary in Lithonia, Georgia.

Currently, he is working on a PhD in Christian Counseling at Louisiana Baptist University.

He also holds several certifications and training in Critical Incident Stress Management, Chaplaincy, Life Coaching, Depression Recovery, and other disciplines.

Don and Kathy are professional life coaches, receiving training from the Professional Christian Coaching Institute.

Don is the CEO of Mingo Coaching Group. He and his wife, Kathy, offer coaching, care, and counsel to leaders worldwide.

Don has severe PTSD plus Facioscapulohumeral Muscular Dystrophy. Learning to deal with these monumental obstacles uniquely enables them to encourage others.

Other Books by Don Mingo

So, You Want to Be A Missionary: Essential
Considerations.

The Cross-Cultural Worker's Spiritual Survival Guide: 14
Survival Tips to Help You Thrive in Your Calling.

A Chrisitan's Mental Health Guide: *For missionaries,
pastors, and Other Christians, too.*

To Hell, Back and Beyond: *A PTSD Journey – When Faith
and Trauma Collide.*

Son Risings: *Discovering and Caring for the Real You.*

Slaying the Dragon Within: *5 Steps to Help Christians Get Out
of Porn – A Discipleship Approach*

Slaying the Dragon Within Workbook in Color: *5 Steps to
Help Christians Get Out of Porn – A Discipleship Approach*

Slaying the Dragon Within Workbook in B & W: *5 Steps
to Help Christians Get Out of Porn – A Discipleship Approach*

The Faith Principle *– 4 Secrets to Making Your Faith Work
Again.*

All books are available through Amazon, Kindle, other book
distributors, or through donmingobooks@gmail.com

[1] Wikimedia Foundation. (2023, October 30). *Smile*. Wikipedia. https://en.wikipedia.org/wiki/Smile#

[2] Gorvett, Z. (2022, February 28). *There are 19 types of smile but only six are for happiness*. BBC Future. https://www.bbc.com/future/article/20170407-why-all-smiles-are-not-the-same

[3] Bhunjun, A. (2022, October 7). *World Smile Day: What's the History? What's The Science of a Smile?* Metro. https://metro.co.uk/2022/10/07/world-smile-day-whats-the-history-whats-the-science-of-a-smile-17521684/

[4] Marmolejo-Ramos, F., Murata, A., Sasaki, K., Yamada, Y., Ikeda, A., Hinojosa, J. A., Watanabe, K., Parzuchowski, M., Tirado, C., & Ospina, R. (2020). Your face and moves seem happier when I smile: Facial action influences the perception of emotional faces and biological motion stimuli. Experimental Psychology, 67(1), 14–22. https://doi.org/10.1027/1618-3169/a000470

[5] Team, B. E. (2023, October 5). *Why Psychologists Study the Duchenne Smile*. BetterHelp. https://betterhelp.com/advice/general/why-psychologists-study-the-duchenne-smile-and-what-it-means-for-you/

[6] Messinger, D. S. F., A. ,. &. Dickson, K. L., Fogel, A., & Dickson, K. L. (n.d.). *What's in a smile?* American Psychological Association. https://psycnet.apa.org/record/1999-05027-009 Developmental Psychology, 35(3), 701–708

[7] Parent, A. (2005, August). *Duchenne de Boulogne: A Pioneer in Neurology and Medical Photography*. The Canadian journal of neurological sciences. Le journal canadien des sciences neurologiques. https://pubmed.ncbi.nlm.nih.gov/16225184/

[8] The Piazza Tales: "A smile is the chosen vehicle of all ambiguities."

[9] Paine, T. (1912). Essay Number 1. In *Common Sense: On the origin and design of government in general, with Concise Remarks on the English Constitution, together with the American CRISIS, 1776-1783* (pp. 176–176). essay, G.P. Putnam's Sons.

[10] Australian Associated Press. (2019, October 9). The *"kindness" quote is not by Mark Twain*. AAP Fact Check. https://www.aap.com.au/factcheck/kindness-quote-is-not-by-mark-twain/

[11] Bovee, C. N. (1857). In *Thoughts, feelings, and fancies* (pp. 109–109). essay, Wiley & Halsted.

[12] Psalms 85:11. NLT

[13] King, F. (n.d.). *Fallen King (thefallenkingof) - profile*. Pinterest. https://www.pinterest.com/TheFallenKingof/

[14] Payne, J. (2021, April 3). *Maj. Dick Winters on adjusting to civilian life after WWII (Band of Brothers)*. YouTube. https://www.youtube.com/watch?v=4wxfmqFw6GM

[15] Hyatt, I. T. (1976). Chapter: Lottie Moon at Shaling and in History. In *Our ordered lives confess: Three nineteenth-century American missionaries in East Shantung* (pp. 123–123). essay, Harvard University Press.

[16] Mikhail, A. (2023, June 28). *Loneliness is a public health crisis, comparable to smoking up to 15 cigarettes a day*. Fortune Well. https://fortune.com/well/2023/06/15/loneliness-comparable-to-smoking-up-to-15-cigarettes-a-day/

[17] Ibid.

[18] Price, R. (2014, March 10). *When loneliness hits*. Mission to the World. https://www.mtw.org/stories/details/when-loneliness-hits

[19] Frazer, S. (2019, June 7). *How the psalms speak to the lonely*. Crosswalk.com. https://www.crosswalk.com/faith/bible-study/how-the-psalms-speak-to-the-lonely.html

[20] Wikimedia Foundation. (2024, April 5). *The Sound of Silence*. Wikipedia. https://en.wikipedia.org/wiki/The_Sound_of_Silence

[21] Nguyen, J. (2023, February 3). *What is chronic loneliness?*. Verywell Mind. https://www.verywellmind.com/what-is-chronic-loneliness-6950783

[22] Shaw, G. (2018, October 9). *9 subtle signs that you're lonely - even if it doesn't feel like it*. Insider. https://www.insider.com/signs-of-loneliness-2018-6

[23] LaRue, J. L. (2023, March 21). *Overcoming signs of loneliness*. Mayo Clinic Health System. https://www.mayoclinichealthsystem.org/hometown-health/speaking-of-health/overcoming-loneliness

[24] Brennan, D. (2021, October 25). *Chronic loneliness: Effects on mental health and ways to treat it*. WebMD. https://www.webmd.com/mental-health/what-to-know-about-chronic-loneliness

[25] O'Donnell, D. S. (2011). Chapter 5: The Devil's Question. In *The Beginning and End of Wisdom: Preaching Christ from the First and Last Chapters of Proverbs, Ecclesiastes, and Job* (eBook, Ser. notes pages 98-100, pp. 199–199). essay, Crossway.

[26] Jeremiah, D. (2023, February 28). *3 ways to overcome loneliness for Christians*. David Jeremiah Blog. https://davidjeremiah.blog/3-ways-to-overcome-loneliness/

[27] R., T. J. R. (2022). *The Lord of the Rings*. William Morrow.

28 Ibid.

29 Definition of "expectancy." (n.d.). *Expectancy definition in American English | Collins English dictionary*. Collins. https://www.collinsdictionary.com/us/dictionary/english/expectancy

30 Ligonier Ministries. (2004, April 29). *Unchangeable things: Reformed bible studies & devotionals at ligonier.org: Reformed Bible Studies & Devotionals at ligonier.org*. Ligonier Ministries. https://www.ligonier.org/learn/devotionals/unchangeable-things#

31 Cambridge English Dictionary. (n.d.). *Apprehension Definition*. Cambridge English Dictionary. https://dictionary.cambridge.org/us/dictionary/english/apprehension

32 Merriam-Webster. (n.d.). *Carpe Diem Definition & Meaning*. Merriam-Webster. https://www.merriam-webster.com/dictionary/carpe%20diem#:~:text=

33 Proverbs 16:18

34 Thompson, P. (202AD, August 18). *What is failure and how can we make the most of it?*. BetterUp. https://www.betterup.com/blog/what-is-failure#

35 Wikimedia Foundation. (2023, September 9). *Failure*. Wikipedia. https://en.wikipedia.org/wiki/Failure

36 Magazine, S. (2017, August 10). *The bizarre story of "Vasa," the ship that keeps on giving*. Smithsonian.com. https://www.smithsonianmag.com/smart-news/bizarre-story-vasa-ship-keeps-giving-180964328/

37 Gorman, S., & Eiras, A. (2023, April 21). *SpaceX rocket explosion illustrates Elon Musk's "successful failure" formula*. Reuters. https://www.reuters.com/lifestyle/science/spacex-rocket-explosion-illustrates-elon-musks-successful-failure-formula-2023-04-20/

38 Kelly, M. (2019, January 28). *3 ways we might misunderstand Romans 8:28*. Forward Progress. https://michaelkelley.co/2019/01/3-ways-we-might-misunderstand-romans-828/

39 YouTube. (2024, February 21). *George Clooney learn from failure #motivation #learning #success*. YouTube. https://www.youtube.com/watch?v=7_-kQF0kvEw

40 *Oxford languages and Google - English*. Oxford Languages. (n.d.). https://languages.oup.com/google-dictionary-en/

41 Allender, D. (2019, October 4). *Entitlement and pride in Psalm 131*. The Allender Center. https://theallendercenter.org/2019/06/psalm-131-entitlement-pride/

42 Dittrich, B. (n.d.). *Bernd Dittrich (@hdbernd): Unsplash Photo Community*. Unsplash Photo Community. https://unsplash.com/@hdbernd

[43] Rachman, S. (2009, December 9). *Betrayal: A psychological analysis*. Behaviour Research and Therapy. https://www.sciencedirect.com/science/article/abs/pii/S0005796709002848

[44] Tayebi, T. (2020, March 20). *The psychology of taking Offense - Fast Company*. These are the reasons why you find something offensive. https://www.fastcompany.com/90472232/these-are-the-reasons-why-you-find-something-offensive

[45] Fries-Gaither, J., & Lockman, A. S. (2020, April 15). *All about icebergs - beyond penguins and polar bears*. Beyond Penguins and Polar Bears . https://beyondpenguins.ehe.osu.edu/issue/icebergs-and-glaciers/all-about-icebergs#

Copyright August 2009 – The Ohio State University. This material is based upon work supported by the National Science Foundation under Grant No. 0733024. Any opinions, findings, and conclusions or recommendations expressed in this material are those of the author(s) and do not necessarily reflect the views of the National Science Foundation. This work is licensed under an Attribution-ShareAlike 3.0 Unported Creative Commons license.

[46] Wikimedia Foundation. (2023c, December 3). *Iceberg*. Wikipedia. https://en.wikipedia.org/wiki/Iceberg#

[47] Vroegop, M. (2022, November 26). *4 ways lament helps missionaries persevere*. Mark Vroegop. https://www.markvroegop.com/blog/kycbkmppymezgawindy2ov1i5mtta4

[48] Kelly, M. (2023, June 27). *Players since 1941 who had .400 within reach*. MLB.com. https://www.mlb.com/news/players-who-came-closest-to-400-since-1941-c197007966

[49] Ibid.

[50] Holtzman, J. (1999, March 7). *Williams: Strikeouts show batters are missing a good thing*. Chicago Tribune. https://www.chicagotribune.com/news/ct-xpm-1999-03-07-9903070427-story.html

[51] Forbes Magazine. (2015). *Thoughts On The Business Of Life*. Quotes. https://www.forbes.com/quotes/11194/

[52] Franklin University. (n.d.). *What do network technicians do: Daily work & skills*. What Do Network Technicians Do: Daily Work & Skills. https://www.franklin.edu/career-guide/computer-network-support-specialists/what-do-network-technicians-do#

[53] MINGO, D. J., & Harty, K. G. CIO (2024, March 8). What Does a Network Technician Do? Personal interview via text messaging.

[54] MINGO, D. J., & Pratt, Steve CIO (2024, June 13). Static, Dynamic, and Hybrid Networking. Calgary; Alberta, Canada.

Steve Pratt: Associate's in electronic engineering ITT Tech A+ Certified Network + Certified ITIL Foundations Certified Microsoft MCITP Certified Senior Systems Email Engineer for 5/3 Bank (2009-2019) Senior Technical Administer for Cintas (2004 – 2009) CEO & Founder of PcConstruct.Net (1997-2003)

[55] Rolf, L. (2023, June 13). *What is data in transit and data at rest*. technology. https://quest-technology-group.com/academy/what-is-data-in-transit-vs-data-at-rest

[56] MINGO, D. J., & Pratt, Steve CIO (2024, June 20). Static, Dynamic, and Hybrid Networking. Calgary; Alberta, Canada.

Steve Pratt: Associate's in electronic engineering ITT Tech A+ Certified Network + Certified ITIL Foundations Certified Microsoft MCITP Certified Senior Systems Email Engineer for 5/3 Bank (2009-2019) Senior Technical Administer for Cintas (2004 – 2009) CEO & Founder of PcConstruct.Net (1997-2003)

[57] Lenovo. (n.d.). *Why are defaults important & how to find the default gateway on your computer*. Why Are Defaults Important & How to Find the Default Gateway on Your Computer | Lenovo US. https://www.lenovo.com/us/en/glossary/default/?orgRef

[58] Wikipedia. (n.d.). *Best-selling desktop computer*. Guinness World Records. https://www.guinnessworldrecords.com/world-records/72695-most-computer-sales

"The Commodore 64, that '80s computer icon, lives again". Archived from the original on December 24, 2014. Retrieved November 17, 2014.

[59] Ibid.

[60] Oxford Global Languages. (n.d.). *Oxford languages and google - english*. Oxford Languages. https://languages.oup.com/google-dictionary-en/

[61] Articles. (2023, August 16). *Dynamic vs. Static Routing*. Wise Systems. https://www.wisesystems.com/blog/dynamic-vs-static-routing-faq/#:

[62] Ibid.

[63] Jacobs, D. (2021, July 6). *Static vs. Dynamic Routing: What is the difference?*. Networking. https://www.techtarget.com/searchnetworking/answer/Static-and-dynamic-routing#:~:text

[64] MINGO, D. J., & Pratt, Steve CIO (2024, June 17). Static, Dynamic, and Hybrid Networking.

[65] Kroger, J. (n.d.). *Paul's dynamic mission principles*. Paul's DYNAMIC MIS-SION PRINCIPLES Guidelines for Missionary Involvement. https://pms-phil.org/wp-content/uploads/2020/07/GO-TEACH-IX-9-Paul-Principles.pdf

[66] Ibid.

[67] Ibid.

[68] Lee, W. M. (2021). *A hybrid Christian Identity in Philippians 1:15-18*. HTS Theological Studies.

https://www.scielo.org.za/scielo.php?script=sci_arttext&pid=S0259-94222021000400009

[69] Speake, J. (2015). In *The Oxford Dictionary of Proverbs* (6th ed., pp. 291–292). essay, Oxford University Press. Attributed to John Ray1627-1705

[70] *G2100 - Euaresteō - Strong's Greek lexicon (KJV)*. Blue Letter Bible. (n.d.). https://www.blueletterbible.org/lexicon/g2100/kjv/tr/0-1/

[71] **The Prosperity gospel** is the teaching in Protestant Christianity that faith—expressed through positive thoughts, declarations, and donations to the church—draws health, wealth, and happiness into believers' lives. It is also referred to as the "health and wealth gospel" or "name it and claim it." Central to this teaching are the beliefs that salvation through Jesus Christ includes liberation from not only death and eternal damnation but also poverty, sickness, and other ills.

Donovan, B. (2023, October 11). *Prosperity gospel*. Encyclopædia Britanica. https://www.britannica.com/topic/prosperity-gospel

[72] Mingo, D. (2020). Chapter 16. In *The Faith Principle: 4 Secrets to Making Your Faith Work For You Again* (pp. 116–117). essay, Mingo Coaching Group.

[73] Ibid.

[74] Unger, M. F., White, W., & Vine, W. E. (1985). Strong's Number: g3406. In *Vine's Expository Dictionary of Biblical Words*. essay, Thomas Nelson Publishers.

[75] Ibid.

[76] Zondervan. (2015). *Bible Gateway passage: 1 Corinthians 10:13 - New International Version*. Bible Gateway. https://www.biblegateway.com/passage/?search=1+Corinthians+10%3A13&version=NIV

NIV Exhaustive Concordance Dictionary. Copyright © 2015 by Zondervan.

[77] *Interlinear search for ' ' - NAS with the BHS and NA26.* StudyLight.org. (n.d.).
https://studylight.org/study-
desk/interlinear.html?q1=1+chronicles%2B21%3A1

[78] *Interlinear search for ' ' - NAS with the BHS and NA26.* StudyLight.org. (n.d.).
https://studylight.org/study-
desk/interlinear.html?q1=1+chronicles%2B21%3A1

[79] MediLexicon International. (n.d.). *Chronic stress: Symptoms, health effects, and how to manage it.* Medical News Today
https://www.addictioncenter.com/alcohol/growing-up-alcoholic-parents-
affects-children/

[80] https://en.wikipedia.org/wiki/Holmes_and_Rahe_stress_scale

[81] https://www.stress.org/holmes-rahe-stress-inventory

[82] Pruett, B. and B. (2012, March 23). *Just how stressed are missionaries (and what can we do about it)?: Brian and Bailey Pruett.* Brian and Bailey Pruett |
Serving in the Philippines with Aviation. Retrieved April 18, 2023, from
https://blogs.ethnos360.org/brian-pruett/2012/03/23/just-how-stressed-are-
missionaries-and-what-can-we-do-about-it/

[83] *Recognizing Stress.* intermountainhealthcare.org. (n.d.).
https://intermountainhealthcare.org/services/wellness-preventive-
medicine/live-well/feel-well/recognizing-stress/

[84] Ducharme, J. (2022, March 8). Watching war unfold on social media affects mental health. Time. Retrieved March 8, 2022, from https://time.com/6155630/ukraine-
war-social-media-mental-health/

[85] Ibid.

[86] Edwards, E. (2022, October 14). Taking a break from the news can improve mental health, study finds. NBCNews.com. Retrieved October 15, 2022, from
https://www.nbcnews.com/health/health-news/taking-break-news-can-improve-
mental-health-study-finds-rcna51954

[87] Grammarist. (n.d.). Retrieved January 7, 2022, from
https://grammarist.com/heteronyms/wound-vs-wound/

[88] Mayo Staff Clinic. (2023, January 7). *Agoraphobia.* Mayo Clinic.
https://www.mayoclinic.org/diseases-conditions/agoraphobia/symptoms-
causes/syc-20355987

[89] Matthews, T., Danese, A., Wertz, J., Ambler, A., Kelly, M., Diver, A., Caspi, A.,
Moffitt, T. E., & Arseneault, L. (2015, March). Social isolation and
mental health at primary and secondary school entry: A longitudinal cohort
study. Journal of the American Academy of Child and Adolescent Psychia-

try. Retrieved March 8, 2022, from https://www.ncbi.nlm.nih.gov/pmc/articles/PMC4733108/

[90] *How growing up with alcoholic parents affects children*. Addiction Center. (2023, January 9). Retrieved January 10, 2023, from https://www.addictioncenter.com/alcohol/growing-up-alcoholic-parents-affects-children/

[91] Atchley, P. (2014, July 23). *You can't multitask, so stop trying*. Managing Yourself. https://hbr.org/2010/12/you-cant-multi-task-so-stop-tr

[92] Yancey, P. (1988). What If. In Disappointment With God (pp. 49–49). essay, Walker & Company.

[93] The great city of the elves in Lord of the Rings.

[94] Powerful demonic monster with powers to shroud itself with darkness in Lord of the Rings.

[95] Department of Health & Human Services. (2001, July 13). *Pain and pain management – adults*. Better Health Channel. https://www.betterhealth.vic.gov.au/health/conditionsandtreatments/pain-and-pain-management-adults

[96] Ibid.

[97] Jones, T. (n.d.). *The 5 coping skills every chronic pain patient needs*. Practical Pain Management. https://aging.idaho.gov/wp-content/uploads/2020/04/PracticalPainManagement_FiveCopingSkills-ChronicPainPatientNeeds.pdf

[98] Ibid.

[99] Ibid.

[100] Ibid.

[101] Ibid. Note source location: Original source: https://www.practicalpainmanagement.com/treatments/complementary/biobeh avioral/5-coping-skills-every-chronic-pain-patient-needs

[102] WebMD. (n.d.). *Drug interaction checker - find interactions between medications*. WebMD. https://www.webmd.com/interaction-checker/default.htm

[103] Spies, P. E., Willems, R., Pot, H., Bos, J. M., & Kramers, C. (2015, August). *Interaction between tramadol and SSRI's: Do we care? - clinical ...* Clinical Therapeutics. https://www.clinicaltherapeutics.com/article/S0149-2918(15)00437-3/fulltext ABSTRACT| VOLUME 37, ISSUE 8, SUPPLEMENT, E43, AUGUST 2015

[104] WebMD. (n.d.). *Drug interaction checker - find interactions between medications.*

[105] Ibid.

[106] Ibid.

[107] Maumus, M., Mancini, R., Zumsteg, D. M., & Mandali, D. K. (2020). Aberrant drug-related behavior monitoring. *Ochsner Journal, 20*(4), 358–361. https://doi.org/10.31486/toj.20.0108

[108] Pain-Outlet Clinical Guide. (n.d.). *5 A's.* PAIN. https://www.pain-outlet.info/5-as.html

[109] Definition of amelioration from the Cambridge Advanced Learner's Dictionary & Thesaurus © Cambridge University Press). (n.d.). *Amelioration definition | Cambridge English Dictionary.* Cambridge.org/. https://dictionary.cambridge.org/us/dictionary/english/amelioration

[110] Center for Medicare and Medicaid Services. (2016, February). *Drug diversion: What is a prescriber's role in preventing ...* Department of Health and Human Services. https://www.hhs.gov/guidance/sites/default/files/hhs-guidance-documents/DrugDiversionFS022316.pdf

[111] Department of Health & Human Services. (2001, July 13). *Pain and pain management – adults.* Better Health Channel. https://www.betterhealth.vic.gov.au/health/conditionsandtreatments/pain-and-pain-management-adults

[112] Monica Foster, Ph. D. (2023, September 7). *Tips for managing chronic pain.* Mayo Clinic Health System. https://www.mayoclinichealthsystem.org/hometown-health/speaking-of-health/8-tips-for-managing-chronic-pain

[113] That will drive a few of you nuts...

[114] MacArthur, J. (1997). Hebrews Chapter 12. In *John MacArthur Study Bible* (p. E. Preserving Faith 12:1-9). essay, Thomas Nelson Publishers.

[115] Jamieson, R. J., Fausset , A. F. R., & Brown , R. J. (AuDavid B. (Author). (n.d.). Hebrews 12. In *Commentary Critical & Explanatory on the Whole* (p. Hebrews 12:1-9-Hebrews 12:4). essay, Life Bible. Public Domain, Life Bible Translation: New Living Translation Life Bible App online at www.lifebible.com

[116] MacArthur, J. (1997). Hebrews Chapter 12. In *John MacArthur Study Bible*

[117] *Life Application Bible: New International Version.* Wheaton, IL: Tyndale, 1991. Print. [Life Application Bible, notes on Hebrews 12:2]

[118] Ibid.

[119] Ibid.

[120] Jameison, R., Fausset, A. R., & Brown, D. (n.d.). Hebrews 12:2-3. In *Life Bible App* (p. Hebrews 12:1-3). essay, Life Bible.com.

[121] Ehrman, B. (2023, March 15). *Why Romans crucified people (the Story Beyond the Cross & Nails)*. The Bart Ehrman Blog. https://ehrmanblog.org/why-romans-crucified-people/

[122] Shaffer, R. (2019). *Jesus was naked when he was crucified. why does he wear a loincloth on the crucifix?*. Quora. https://www.quora.com/Jesus-was-naked-when-he-was-crucified-Why-does-he-wear-a-loincloth-on-the-crucifix

[123] Ehrman, B. (2023b, July 25). *Did Romans allow decent burials for crucified criminals?*. The Bart Ehrman Blog. https://ehrmanblog.org/did-romans-allow-decent-burials-for-crucified-criminals/

[124] Mission Discovery. (2023, June 1). *What is living water?* https://www.missiondiscovery.org/news/what-does-the-bible-mean-about-streams-of-living-water/

Made in the USA
Middletown, DE
03 September 2024

60299325R00116